Best wishes!

Larry Scheckel

Other Books by Larry Scheckel

Ask Your Science Teacher

I Always Wondered About That: 101 Questions and Answers About Science and Other Stuff

Seneca Seasons: A Farm Boy Remembers

Ask A Science Teacher

I Always Wondered About That Too: 111 Questions and Answers About Science and Other Stuff (November, 2018)

I Just Keep Wondering About That: 121 Questions and Answers About Science and Other Stuff (2019)

MURDER
in Wisconsin
THE Clara Olson CASE

LARRY SCHECKEL

OAK
GROVE
PRESS

Murder in Wisconsin: The Clara Olson Case

Copyright © Larry Scheckel, 2018

All right reserved. No portion of this book may be reproduced, distributed, or transmitted in any form or by any means electronic or mechanical, including photocopying, recording, or information storage or retrieval system, without the prior written permission of the publisher.

If you would like to do any of the above, please seek permission by contact us at lscheckel@charter.net.

Thanks to Adept Concept Solutions for formatting the manuscript.

Published by:
Oak Grove Press
1113 Parkview Dr.
Tomah, WI 54660
https://larryscheckel.com

Published in the United States.
978-1-7322765-1-2

*This book is dedicated to our parents,
Alvin and Martha Scheckel and Leonard and Loretta Martin.
They taught us the true meaning of everyday love.*

Contents

	Foreword	ix
	Introduction	xiii
CHAPTER 1	Love in the Hill Country	1
CHAPTER 2	Close to the Land	7
CHAPTER 3	Clara Olson in Love	17
CHAPTER 4	The Dog Days of August	27
CHAPTER 5	Erdman Olson Mulls His Options	35
CHAPTER 6	A Fateful Day	41
CHAPTER 7	Murder in the Hill Country	47
CHAPTER 8	The Morning After	53
CHAPTER 9	Clara is Missing	61
CHAPTER 10	Missing Girl Is Big News	69
CHAPTER 11	Clara Olson Found Dead	77
CHAPTER 12	How Did She Die?	85
CHAPTER 13	The Autopsy	93
CHAPTER 14	The District Attorney Acts	103

CHAPTER 15	**Two Families, Two Views**	111
CHAPTER 16	**The Pathologist Uncovers a Secret**	123
CHAPTER 17	**The Questioning Continues**	137
CHAPTER 18	**The Verdict**	153
CHAPTER 19	**Laying Clara to Rest**	163
CHAPTER 20	**The News Spreads to the World**	171
CHAPTER 21	**The Search for a Killer**	181
CHAPTER 22	**Grasping at Straws**	191
CHAPTER 23	**Erdman's Parents Demand a Review**	203
CHAPTER 24	**The Trail Goes Cold**	209
	Epilogue	215
	Timeline	223
	Acknowledgments	227
	People Involved	229

Foreword

Murder in Wisconsin is an intriguing account of an intense love affair of two young people that involves all the clichés, all the popular events of the time, and all the tragedy that usually is only seen in the movies. Larry Scheckel has captured this true story with intense feeling, a feeling that many people have experienced in the last ninety years since the murder. The feeling of knowing a daughter has disappeared, the feeling of having a son accused of murder, the feelings of neighbors finding the body, and the feeling that the murderer will never be found. And, certainly, the feeling you get while standing in that very woods, looking at the indentation in the ground, and reliving in your mind what could possibly have ever happened that would end like this?

My family and Larry's family have ties to Crawford County, to Seneca High School, and to the rural areas. Our families have known each other for the last fifty-plus years with all of our siblings attending Seneca High School. His book, *Seneca Seasons*, brings back many memories. It touches on the lives of all the families in the area, and tells the story of a family, that in many ways, was what life was all about in Crawford County.

Larry has shown the same intensity in *Murder in Wisconsin*. His book reveals a young girl, typical of her time, living in a home with a good family, yet wanting something more. The book tells you of a young man, perhaps not so typical, but with a good home and family, but wanting something very different than his girlfriend. It will take you through their story and leave you with the same intense interest that has intrigued so many over the last ninety years. It will show you why it gained national attention.

Larry has made numerous trips to Crawford County to interview people and read media reports and has brought together all that information in this first book on the Clara Olson murder.

Having lived in the Rising Sun area, going to the Rising Sun Grade School, and being friends of some of the relatives of the Olson families, naturally we were curious about this when we were kids. As kids, my friend Rodney Hanson and I would ride our bikes down the highway, take the trail into the woods, and look at the grave site. Scary? Yes. Did we do it more than once? You bet.

Three girls from Fairview walked into the woods, found a Sir Walter Raleigh tobacco can, opened it, screamed, and ran out of there. Never returning!

My parents and aunts and uncles were of the same generation as the two Olson families. They were friends and neighbors. We never thought too much about asking them questions. Once in a while, they would mention something. But seldom. This book will answer those questions. It will tell you what the police knew, what the media knew, and what friends and neighbors knew. It will show you why so many of us have been intrigued by the "open murder case" on Battle Ridge.

Roger Forde

MURDER
in Wisconsin

Introduction

When my two brothers and I were young lads, Dad would take us to Rising Sun, a few miles east of the Mississippi River, to get our hair cut. At that time, haircuts cost 50 cents for kids. Into the barber shop we trooped. Bernie Hanson's Barber Shop was a one-chair, first come, first cut facility. It was actually a shack, half the size of a one-car garage. Dad got his hair cut first, paid for all four haircuts, and retired for a beer or two at Crowley's, the tavern next door. One by one, Phillip, Bob, and I got our haircuts and then went next door for a special treat of a frosty glass of soda pop.

One evening in the summer of 1954, motoring south from Rising Sun toward Mt. Sterling on Highway 27, Dad pointed over into the woods and said, "That's where they found that Olson girl. She was murdered and buried there." The three of us had never heard the story, so Dad gave us a brief account.

I was intrigued. A murder scene right outside our black 1940 Chevrolet. I asked Dad, "Can we stop and look at it?" Dad replied, "No, it's dark and the grave hole is probably caved in after 30 years."

My fascination with the story of Clara Olson continued throughout my life. Recently, when I researched the story, I discovered that it was the murder of the century for Crawford County, if not all of southwestern Wisconsin.

Newspapers all over the world covered the story of the Clara Olson murder. The coverage began with Crawford County's local newspaper, the *Courier Press*, founded in 1868. Slightly farther afield, the *La Crosse Tribune and Leader-Press* and the *Winona Republican-Herald* began covering it. The interest spread outward to the *Chicago Herald-Examiner*, the *Chicago Tribune*, and the *Milwaukee Sentinel*, all of which sent reporters and photographers by train to the county seat of Prairie du Chien. Even *the New York Times* covered it.

The account in this book is taken from newspaper accounts, historical archives, printed testimony, recollections of relatives, and stories passed down through several generations.

As I realized very quickly, newspapers of that era did not observe the highest levels of scrupulous detail. It was the heyday of tabloid journalism. Stories and episodes, no matter how peripheral, were hyped as newsworthy. No matter how thin the facts, they printed whatever they thought would sell papers. Sensationalist accounts were plentiful. Human interest stories, designed to tug at the heartstrings, utilized melodrama to the nth degree. Reporters did not let the facts get in the way of a good story.

The Clara Olson murder saga has all the elements of high drama: passion, betrayal, murder, denial, and flight. It is a mystery worthy of the best detectives. After ninety years, this gruesome murder remains one of the most talked-about crimes in the history of Wisconsin.

Any writer doing research on a historical event will encounter errors and contradictions. Such is the case in the murder of Clara Olson. Yet, despite several inaccuracies, I was able to piece together the story. The research data lined up reasonably well.

I was also able to visit all of the sites covered in the newspaper accounts. A drive down through Crawford County on the Black River Road, Highway 27, reveals a countryside virtually unchanged since 1926.

I have taken that highway often, visiting my parents who lived their retirement years in the village of Seneca. As I head south on Highway 27, my heart quickens when I get to Rising

Sun, just inside Crawford County, where a flood of many fond memories comes gushing forth. I have moved into the land and the people I know so well.

Motoring a few miles south of Rising Sun I see the "place where they found that Olson girl" as Dad pointed out to us decades earlier. The burial site, a small depression on the wooded hillside, is still there, its exact location known only to a few. I park the car along the side of the highway, walk in, and view the depression from which searchers discovered her body on December 2, 1926. It is a sad quiet place; the only sounds are squirrels scurrying about, the wind in the trees and the clatter of machinery on distant farms.

Back in the car, I drive a few hundred yards to the south, and around a bend in the road and off to the left is the driveway to the farmstead that belonged to Albert and Anna Olson and sons Erdman and Arvid.

Continuing south on Highway 27, I slow down for the community of Fairview, population 13. The most distinctive feature is a that of a half-dozen tractors, mostly Minneapolis Moline, parked right beside the highway, waiting to be restored.

I pull into the driveway of Utica Lutheran Church. From our hill pasture out on Oak Grove Ridge, we could look a bit east of north and see the steeple of Utica Lutheran Church.

The Utica Lutheran Church is Norwegian Lutheran. Names on the grave markers read: Anderson, Aspenson, Enerson, Gunderson, Monson, Halverson, Hjelle, and Knutson.

I go to the cemetery. I walk over to the grave of Clara Olson, the young lady who was murdered. Her parents, Chris and Dina Olson, were also laid to rest here. Most of Clara's siblings are also interred in the Utica Lutheran Church Cemetery. It is a most peaceful and serene setting, one of the highest places in Crawford County. From the cemetery, Battle Ridge, the site of Clara's murder can be seen to the north.

Next, I drive to the village of Mt. Sterling, population 200, which was named after Will Sterling. William T. Sterling, at age 19, came up to Wisconsin from his birthplace in Kentucky, along with Henry Dodge, to make some money in the lead mines of southwestern Wisconsin.

Now I am approaching Stony Point on Highway 27. A road leading west from Stony Point is the road leading to the Chris Olson farm, where Clara was raised. Young Clara Olson would walk over from here to the Lynch family farm to help with the domestic chores of washing clothes, cooking, and tending small children.

Next, I come to Seneca, named after a Seneca in New York State. Langdon built a hotel here, and the road thru Seneca became known as the Black River Road.

Seneca was originally a stagecoach stop. It had a blacksmith shop, trading post, drug store, shoemaker, harness shop, and wagon maker. Seneca was home to the Neil Tollefson Hall, with a hotel and pool hall on the first floor, and the dance hall on the second floor. In 1926, this dance hall made national headlines because Erdman Olson left this dance hall around 11 p.m. on the night of September 9, 1926 to meet Clara Olson. She was never seen alive again.

Within the pages of this book, you will discover Clara Olson's fascinating story and the events that ultimately led up to her tragic end.

*Clara Olson was a 21-year-old beauty,
leading a quiet life as a farm worker and domestic.*

CHAPTER 1

Love in the Hill Country

Crawford County lies in the very heart of the Driftless area, a region encompassing parts of Wisconsin, Minnesota, Iowa, and Illinois. "Driftless" is the expanse of the countryside that the glaciers did not pass over and hence did not leave the sediment material referred to as "drift" in this area. The French, who came here in the 1600s, named it "coulee" country, meaning, "to flow." It is a steep, rugged landscape where numerous coldwater streams cut deeply into the ancient bedrock. The inhabitants simply call it the hill country.

Drifter would become the epitaph for Erdman Olson, one of the young lovers in this tale. He was the son of wealthy tobacco farmers, Albert and Anna Olson, who lived near Rising Sun. He was 18 years old and a student at Gale College in Galesville, north of La Crosse, when he met Clara Olson in the early summer of 1925 at a Lutheran church social.

Clara, nearly four years older, was an attractive farm girl, and she was smitten by the handsome, wealthy, worldly young man. Clara had never traveled much. She had taken the train to Milwaukee to visit friends a few years earlier. She had been to La Crosse but one time.

That was not unusual for the residents of "Little Norway." Her father, Christian Bottolf Olson, was in fact born in

Hornindal, Sogn og Fjordane, Norway. He immigrated to the United States in 1885, at age 18. Her mother, Dina Sandwik, was born in the old country in 1871, and she got off the boat in 1891. On October 29, 1892, Chris and Dina were married in La Crosse, when he was 24 years old and she was 21.

Their first child, Minnie, was born the same year, a late Christmas present, on December 28, 1892. That means Dina was seven months pregnant at the time of the wedding. This practice was quite common at the time. No need for a "shotgun wedding." Nine children would follow.

Adolph was born in 1894, Bernard in 1886, and Emma in 1898. Arthur was born in 1901, but only lived for six weeks. A second Arthur J. was born in 1902. A common practice at the time was to use the name of a deceased child for a newborn, sort of a replacement child.

Four baby girls followed: Clara on September 12, 1904, Alice in 1907, Cornelia in 1910, and Inga in 1913. All the children were born at home, with the assistance of a midwife, just as all the other babies that came into the world on the farms and villages of Crawford County.

Nine of the ten children reached adulthood, a high success rate at a time when life was precious and capricious in rural southwest Wisconsin. Cemetery markers attested to a troubling percentage of children that never reached adulthood. Mothers and babies died in childbirth. The diseases of diphtheria, polio, tuberculosis, and influenza were widespread, gnawing at the conscience, instilling fears. Only a few years before, the Great Influenza Pandemic of 1918–1920 had taken 50 to 100 million lives worldwide and 650,000 Americans. Children would skip rope to a grim rhyme:

> *"I had a little bird.*
> *Its name was Enza.*
> *I opened the window,*
> *And in-flu-enza."*

Most of the Norwegians who emigrated to Crawford County settled in the four northern townships of Seneca, Freeman, Utica, and Clayton. Those that settled in Utica were from five counties in Norway; Luster, Aardal, Borgund, Laerdal and Sunnfjord.

The Norwegians took the high ground on which to build a church. The home congregation for the Chris Olson family was the Utica Lutheran Church, set on a rise on Black River Road, about halfway between the villages of Rising Sun and Mt. Sterling. Anyone standing in the gravel parking lot across the road from Utica Lutheran has a commanding view of the farms and fields of the Driftless area. The gleaming white steeple can be spotted for miles around. A walk through the cemetery attests to the Norse linkage: Helgerson, Kvigne, Tollefson, and Vedvik.

The Utica Congregation was organized in March 13, 1871, at the home of Paul Hansen Helland. A decision was made to build a church, and that was dedicated on May 19, 1881. In 1905 the new church organ was purchased. Ironically, that same year Erdman's father, Albert Olson, married Anna O. Severson there on July 12. The Albert Olson family later switched churches.

Clara grew up to be a home-loving beauty much admired by the boys of the countryside. One of them was a college lad, dapper, a fast talker who had his own car, plenty of money to spend, and an air of sophistication lacking in the lads of the rugged farmland.

Although Erdman was not related to Clara, his roots were very similar. His grandfather, Andrew C. Olson, was born October 2, 1845, and immigrated from Norway. The roster of Company K, 50th Regiment of the Wisconsin Voluntary Infantry, serving in the Civil War, lists his last name as Oleson, from Freeman, enlisted on April 6, 1865, and mustered out on June 14, 1866. He married Ellen Amundson, and they had a lone son named Albert Emil Olson. Albert was born near Kindred, North Dakota, near the Minnesota line, on August 7, 1883.

Four years later, the family moved to the township of Utica in Crawford County.

Albert Olson married Anna O. Severson at Viroqua on July 12, 1905. Apparently, they moved back to North Dakota, as the firstborn of this union was Erdman Sanford Olson, born on July 22, 1908. Erdman was baptized at St. John's Lutheran Church in Ryder, North Dakota, on October 4, 1908. The young family soon moved back to Wisconsin, where a second boy, Arvid, was born on June 4, 1915.

Albert and Anna raised tobacco on 280 acres of good Wisconsin farmland. They became sufficiently well-to-do that they could afford two cars and send Erdman off to Gale College at age 16, at a time when ages for higher education were younger. Before then Erdman attended the one-room Tully School country school near Rising Sun. Gale, a college owned by the Norwegian Evangelical Lutheran Church, was for the sons of those who could afford it. Graduates were expected to be ministers, lawyers, and leaders of their community.

The members of the Albert Olson family frequented the South West Prairie Lutheran Church just north of the Crawford County line in Vernon County. The white wood-frame church is set among beautiful rolling hills, a patchwork of cultivated fields and wood lots.

In such a setting Erdman would meet Clara, and the two fell in love. Of all of Clara's siblings, her sister Alice, three years younger, was closest to her. According to a later story in the *Chicago Herald-Examiner*, writer Patricia Dougherty quoted Alice, Clara's sister, recalling the first time the couple had met.

"Clara met Erdman at a basket social at Peter Severson's a year and a half ago. She fell in love with him the minute she saw him, she told me afterward. I was at a party with a boy from Mt. Sterling and we four came home together. Erdman kept talking about Clara's pretty eyes. He was a quite a smart fellow to hear talk, and I could tell from the way Clara looked at him that she was believing everything he said. She used to fuss with her clothes and make new things to wear when he came. When they found her body, there was a bottle of perfume in her purse that she had sent to La Crosse for, one time when she was expecting him to come home from school. She loved him all right. She used to sit for hours holding his letters and reading them over and over. But I guess he wasn't man enough to appreciate her."

Clara met Erdman on June 25, 1925. She has 441 days to live.

(Top) *Tobacco was the king crop in the first half of the twentieth century in southwest Wisconsin.*
(Bottom) *Tobacco was such a lucrative crop it was often referred to as the "mortgage lifter."*

CHAPTER 2

Close to the Land

Sunday, June 21, 1925, would turn out to be a pivotal day for both Erdman Olson and Clara Olson. The day dawned warm with ample moisture in the air. Later in the afternoon it would be described as "hot and muggy." Farm families kept a leery eye to the sky, mindful of the devastating tri-state tornado that tore through Missouri, Illinois, and Indiana just a few months before, killing nearly 700 people.

The portent of bad weather did not prevent farm families from attending the basket social on the Peter Severson farm near Utica Lutheran Church on Highway 27. What circumstances brought these two young people together? Clara's family attended the Utica Lutheran Church, and Erdman's family attended to the South West Prairie Lutheran Church. Erdman Olson's mother was Anna Severson, and Anna and Peter were related. It is only natural that Clara and Erdman would meet, even though they attended different churches.

Farm families looked forward to the fun of school programs, trips to town, church gatherings, and other social events. Chautauqua was an adult educational movement in the United States, typically held outdoors in tents. Chautauqua events drew huge crowds for lectures, speakers, preachers, plays, musical concerts, and other cultural entertainment, and everyone looked forward to July 4th fireworks. Farm folks enjoyed going to the county fair in Gays Mills and Viroqua in the summer,

Budgets were terribly tight, and farmers were very frugal. They didn't like paying taxes, and, heaven forbid, spending money for anything that was not absolutely necessary. The goal of the basket social was to raise a little extra money for the church to use for nonbudgeted items, such as kitchen provisions, cleaning supplies, and new hymnals. The Norwegian Lutheran church basket socials were patterned along the same lines as those held by many of the one-room schools in the area.

Families were informed several weeks in advance. The minister stressed the importance of raising money and, perhaps not coincidentally, held out the promise of homemade ice cream. The blanket raffle was the big fund-raiser. The blanket was a result of the many quilting parties held the previous winter. One chance cost ten cents or three chances for a quarter.

Every mother and adult daughter prepared a lunch—sandwiches, fruit, brownies, cookies—and put them in a paper bag or picnic basket. All the farmers, their wives, and children arrived between seven to eight o'clock or whenever the milking was done.

The basket social on that day was held on the farm of Peter Severson, a prominent elder of the Utica Lutheran Church. Erdman Olson, on summer vacation after one year at Gale College, arrived in his own car, a new Ford Roadster. Clara came with her parents. The naïve farm girl was smitten by the handsome, wealthy, worldly young man. A chance encounter that would spell disaster for both.

Although both young lovers hailed from nearby farms, their lifestyles were quite different. Erdman's father, Albert, was a successful man who had enough wealth to send his elder son to college. Clara's family was more common, making a living because everyone pitched in with the endless chores around the farm.

At this time farmers were a significant part of the labor force in the United States, adding up to 27 percent. Stark differences yawned open between the social, economic, and cultural lives of big city residents and Wisconsin farm families.

On Clara's farm there was no electricity. Like most folks in the hill country of Crawford County, they still used kerosene lanterns and lamps.

Few farms had indoor plumbing. The standard receptacle was a "one-holer" outhouse. The previous year's Sears catalog, with its thin black-and-white pages, was used as toilet paper. A chamber pot, kept in several rooms, saved a walk outside in stormy or bitterly cold winter weather. The "one-holer" was a frequent target of pranksters, who deemed it their duty to tip a few over each Halloween.

Refrigerators might be enjoyed by city dwellers in the 1920s, but not on Wisconsin farms. The icebox was still the primary way to keep food cold, filled with ice cut from the frozen lakes in the wintertime and stored in sawdust. A block of ice could be kept intact nearly all summer.

Most rural houses had little insulation and were frigid if anyone stood more than 10 feet from the wood-burning stoves. Those stoves were used year-round for cooking and heating water for baths. Few second floors had any heat, and water would freeze if left in the open. Kids kept cozy under many layers of sheets and blankets.

During the hot months of June, July, August, and on into September, a "summer kitchen" was set up. The separate small building close to the house contained a second stove or the stove moved out from the main house. This prevented the fires used for cooking from further heating a house that had no air conditioning and perhaps not even a fan.

Like most farm girls, Clara dutifully went about her daily routine. Milking cows in the morning. Then breakfast. During the long hot summer days, hoeing weeds in the tobacco fields. Blistering sun, flies, and mosquitoes. Cooking, washing dishes, washing and ironing clothes, mending, sitting on the porch in the cool of the evening. Sewing was done on a treadle machine, power provided by the sewing machine operator's foot. There were the never-ending tasks of darning, stitching, and making clothes made from cloth feed bags and seed bags.

She had been taught in a one-room country school, one of 115 rural schools in Crawford County in the 1920s. No child, decreed the lawmakers, should have to walk more than two miles to attend school. This was where Clara would have attended her first basket social. Three events bound farm families together in their county schools: the basket social in the fall, the Christmas program, and the end-of-the-year picnic.

Another joyous occasion during the year occurred shortly after Clara first met Erdman. Threshing day was a big deal on every farm. Each farmer had already run their horse-drawn grain binder through the fields and put the bundles into shocks. A dozen or more farmers with their teams of horses and wagons would then load the grain bundles onto wagons, park next to the behemoth thresher, and pitch the bundles in the gnawing mouth of a hungry machine, separating the oats from the stalks. Such a threshing ring allowed one farmer to own an expensive threshing machine, moving the machine from farm to farm, and charging a fee to thresh the grain. The farm women came together to fix a hearty noon meal for the threshing crew. This was a time to socialize and catch up on the news of neighboring families.

The threshing machine was but one innovation in this era of transition for farms across the Midwest. For the first time, commercial fertilizer was being used to supplement manure. The first hybrid seed corn company was organized. Farmers were making the transition from horse-drawn plows to steel-wheeled tractors, albeit slowly. Although steam- and gasoline-powered tractors had been available for several years, few farmers wanted or could afford these big, heavy machines in the early 1920s. A smaller, lighter tractor had been developed by 1926, but no smart farmer got rid of his horses in those times.

The lives of Wisconsin farmers during this decade were more profoundly transformed by the gasoline-powered automobile and truck, where the advantage was especially acute in sparsely populated areas. A car or truck meant mobility. No need to harness and hitch up a team of horses to go to town. A few hand cranks on a Model T Ford, hop in, and head off to Seneca, or Mt. Sterling, or Rising Sun. Maybe to a big city like Prairie du Chien, with its population of over 3,500.

By 1920, half the cars in America were Ford Model Ts, and a new one could be had for as little as $415. Henry Ford said you could buy a Model T in any color you want "as long as it was black." Why black? The Ford engineers knew that black was the fastest drying paint.

These drivers didn't care that most roads were simply dirt paths—dusty in dry weather, muddy tracks in the rain, and creased with frozen ruts in the winter. Cars driving over such roads took a terrible pounding. Particularly for younger people, none of that interfered with the tremendous feeling of freedom that a car gave them.

Among them was Erdman Olson. His Ford Roadster created all sorts of opportunities as he motored through the countryside. He found all the dances for miles around. He took the girls he met for a spin. He even transported booze in this age of Prohibition.

With his wealth and mobility, he was far more aware of the glitter of the Roaring Twenties. The gangland crime, flapper fashions, dance marathons, and Jazz Age glamour might be far away from the sunrise-to sunset-labor of Crawford County farmers. Yet he would go to the movie houses that were being opened in small towns across America. Prairie du Chien had one, and La Crosse had several, showing the silent black-and-white films featuring Rudolph Valentino and Mary Pickford.

During his visits to these small cities he would also become accustomed to their paved streets, municipal electricity and water distributions, telephone exchanges, streetlights, and sewage systems. The homes of most houses in La Crosse had running water and indoor plumbing. Electricity appeared in homes on a grand scale during the 1920s, at first for illumination but by the end of the decade for washing or sewing machines, irons, toasters, mixers, and vacuum cleaners. Refrigerators began to replace iceboxes for short-term food preservation, and electric fans cooled folks on hot summer days.

Change came more slowly for country people, who would wait another decade or two for electric appliances. More prosperous farmers had a Delco-Light portable 32-volt electric generator powered by a gasoline engine. The generator ran a few hours a day and charged a series of batteries that were used to power lights and appliances. More prosperous farmers owned a small gasoline engine that powered a wringer-washer. Yet water was still pumped from a cistern and carried by pail into the house. The lady of the house still hung out the wash on an outdoor clothesline. Ironing clothes was a common evening chore.

While Erdman might consider himself more sophisticated than his new girlfriend, they were both bound by age-old traditions that governed the growing season. In the counties of Vernon and Crawford, that especially applied to tobacco. It was so important as a cash crop it was nicknamed the "mortgage lifter." In some old pictures, the tobacco sheds look better kept than the house. The house didn't pay the bills, and neither did the row crops.

The unglaciated ridges and valleys of the two counties made excellent tobacco land. The glaciers of the ice age didn't reach into southwest Wisconsin, leaving it with seven-to-eight feet of black dirt that had been wind-blown into the area from the west over thousands of years.

Raising tobacco was an intensive family project. Seeds were planted in seed beds, with young plants pulled out and prepared to be inserted in a planting machine pulled by a team of horses. Several acres could be planted this way, but farmers with up to 50 acres of tobacco counted heavily on outside help, hired hands, and borrowed or rented equipment.

May was the traditional month for planting tobacco in the region. Once a field was planted, it had to be tended, with regular hoeing to remove weeds. While tobacco could bring a big profit, a crop could be destroyed by worms or by a hailstorm. Farmers could buy crop insurance, but it was expensive, and few farmers did. They just prayed to God and took their chances.

Tobacco growing is very labor-intensive, taking much time and energy. Some tobacco farmers could not keep the fences repaired, buildings painted, weeds mowed, and cattle attended to. Other crops suffered.

As the tobacco plant grows, "topping" and "suckering" are required. Topping is the removal of the tobacco flowers so the plant does not pollinate and go to seed, and suckering is the process of pruning leaves that are otherwise unproductive. These two measures help the plant to focus its energy on producing the large leaves that are harvested and sold. The terms for removing the unproductive leaves were "cropping," "pulling," and "priming."

After a 60-day growing season, mature tobacco plants are harvested, taken to sheds, and hung on laths so the plants would dry. It was not uncommon for up to four different levels of workers to be hanging tobacco in a shed, passing the laths to greater heights. After that, the harvested tobacco had to be cured and aged. Cut leaves are hung in bundles in a barn or shed for a minimum of four weeks. Only then would it be ready for consumption in cigars, pipes, or by chewing.

"When it came to harvest time, people who had moved away would take their vacation and come back to Vernon and Crawford Counties to help their families out with the crop," one old-timer reminisced. "I guess for some it wasn't much fun getting a backache on their vacation, but it was a time when the whole family would come together, and some people wouldn't miss it for the world."

Tobacco, hanging in the shed, dried and turned color from green to brown. Farmers waited for "casing weather," warm and humid days, around late December or early January. The humidity would soften the leaves and prepare them for stripping. The laths would be brought down from the shed, and the leaves would be stripped from the stalk and then baled in a stripping box. The tobacco could then be sent to a warehouse. Tobacco can be properly stored in a warehouse for up to 10 years.

"I love it when it's hanging in the shed. It feels like velvet, just before stripping, and it smells really good. It smells like money," was a common sentiment of tobacco growers. "When the tobacco checks came in, you could see it downtown."

Wisconsin had two tobacco-producing areas: a Northern Pool and a Southern Pool. In the northern area, Viroqua was the hub for everything about tobacco for the better part of a century. It was the home to the Northern Wisconsin Cooperative

Tobacco Pool. All tobacco farmers in the northern area belong to the pool, which was basically a co-op through which their tobacco was priced and sold. The pool also administered the allotments of land on which farmers are allowed to grow tobacco.

On the Albert Olson farm, a few miles south of Rising Sun, the tobacco crop supported their wealth. Their older son, Erdman, went sent away to study at Gale College. Younger son Arvid, age 11, helped when he was not at the Tully one-room country school, a half mile south of the farmstead. Hired hand Edwin Knutson and several other seasonal workers put in the crop.

On the Chris Olson farm, a few miles north of Seneca, the entire family would put in the tobacco crop in the spring. For Clara Olson, such a chore did not sour the brightness she felt inside. She was in love. Although Erdman was four years younger and not yet out of college, she could not be blamed for thinking that marriage would soon follow.

On September 8, 1925, Erdman Olson is enrolled in Gale College, Galesville, Wisconsin. Clara Olson tends her chores and tasks on the Chris Olson farm. Clara has 366 days to live.

(Left) *Erdman, 18, was charged in the 1926 slaying of his sweetheart, Clara Olson (no relation). Erdman, the eldest son of wealthy tobacco growers, would take out Clara while home from college. They went to dances together and often on long automobile rides. After Clara's disappearance, her father visited Erdman at Gale College and pleaded with him to return his daughter. A few days after the visit, the young man disappeared from college and was never seen again.*
(Top right) *Utica Lutheran Church was the home church of the Chris Olson family. Clara Olson was confirmed in this church, attended many services and socials, and was buried from this church.*
(Middle right) *Southwest Prairie Lutheran Church is typical of the Norwegian Lutheran Churches that dot Crawford and Vernon Counties of southwestern Wisconsin.*
(Bottom right) *Southwest Prairie Lutheran Church was the home parish of the Albert Olson family. Southwest Prairie is in Vernon County, just north of the Crawford County and Vernon County line.*

CHAPTER 3

Clara Olson in Love

He dressed fastidiously, seemed to have lots of money, and was described as a snappy-dressed college boy, with an aura of sophistication. He had his own car, a Ford Roadster. The hill country was abuzz about his fast living and illegal booze. Young Erdman knew who had the stuff, and he had the money to purchase it. There was no Prohibition for many farm youths of the mid-1920s.

The rebelliousness native to teenagers had an obvious target back in this era. The Volstead Act of 1919, the Eighteenth Amendment as it was officially named, had outlawed alcohol. A great experiment had begun: improve man and society by regulating the use of alcohol. Temperance supporters claimed that Prohibition would put an end to families living in poverty, as the breadwinner wouldn't be tossing his wages into the urinal. People would no longer get drunk and kill other people. In Crawford County, Norwegian Lutheran minsters had been railing against the evil brew for decades. They were delighted to see the end of "John Barleycorn."

Their parishioners were hardly as adamant. In fact, Wisconsin residents of German, Italian, Polish, and Irish descent hated Prohibition with a vengeance. Erdman Olson was an enthusiastic member of that faction. He carried a stainless steel six-ounce whiskey flask, contoured to fit the rump if carried in the back pocket, hence the name "hip flask." Or the chest area if conveyed inside a suit coat. Most flasks had a "captive top," which consisted of a small arm that attaches to the top of the flask in order to stop it from getting lost when it was taken off. Cheaper flasks were made of pewter, but that did not fit Erdman Olson. He went for the best.

The liquor flask was not just the prerogative of men. The not-so-nice ladies transported the flask against the thigh, held in place by a garter. A popular model sported the words "VOTE NO ON LIQUOR," an in-your-face tribute to the Temperance League ladies.

Besides snubbing their noses at the unpopular Eighteenth Amendment, flask patrons greeted strangers as a sign of camaraderie and friendship. It bolstered grooms at the altar. Candidates handed out flasks with their campaign slogans printed boldly on the side, with a reminder to be sure to vote for the right person.

It is not surprising the Erdman Olson carried a flask of hooch to dances and parties. One can only speculate if his father and mother had any knowledge of their son's flaunting the law. Or to the dangers to the family reputation or his standing at Gale College.

The flask was part of Erdman's image. He was described as a Don Juan country boy. Erdman's father had a lot of money—wads of cash, people said. Albert Olson was an only child, and he had inherited everything from his parents. Over and over, newspapers would later report Albert as "a wealthy tobacco farmer." Erdman was the oldest of two boys and stood to inherit everything, and he knew it. It shaped his behavior, especially his superiority complex.

The girls in central Crawford County knew Erdman, and he knew all of them. The *Winona Republican Herald* would later discover that he had girls at college as well. "While at college, Olson often kept company with Luella Christiansen and Ella Rude. Whether one of these was the girl whom Erdman is said to have written two special delivery letters a week during the summer vacation, could not be learned."

He would arrive at a dance in his car and flash plenty of spending money. He carried a flask of moonshine in his back pocket, and he would show the booze at dances. The other young men would plunk down a few bucks for the stuff. They didn't know where he got it, but he always had some.

His sources were not hard to find. The Volstead Act of 1919 had not outlawed the drinking of alcohol, just its manufacture and sale. "No person shall manufacture, sell, barter, transport, import, export, deliver, or furnish any intoxicating liquor." As a result, the country was "dry," but in fact lots of people continued to drink. Many a farmer up and down the hills and valleys of the Kickapoo River, Rush Creek, Sugar Creek, Kettle Hollow, and Hobbs Hollow tended a still on the sly.

They were replacing a thriving industry. Wisconsin had lost nearly 10,000 taverns. Milwaukee breweries laid off 6,000 employees. In the breech stepped Norwegian farmers, setting up their own little brew operation along the creeks and in the hollows in the rugged country of the unglaciated Driftless area. Why not make a little money on the side? Perhaps expand the farm operation. Buy a new tractor, a newer car, fix up the house the way the wife had been begging for years. Indoor plumbing, a refrigerator, even a better team of horses? A farmer might stroll down in the valley and check out the still after milking cows in the evening and after working all day in the tobacco fields.

Storekeepers in Rising Sun, Mt. Sterling, Seneca, and Gays Mills were quite discreet whenever a farmer requested a dozen feet of copper piping or a large copper kettle. After all, the same copper kettle could be used for making apple butter or hold the wash on laundry day.

The farmer owned the raw materials. Corn mash was put in a copper kettle and left to ferment. After an allotted amount of time, a wood fire heated up the liquid so it became a vapor. That ran through a water-cooled coil of copper pipes to condense the vapor into good liquor. The running creeks supplied the cool water needed to condense the steam back into liquor.

"Running a still" was breaking the law, but you had to get caught first, and nobody talked, and the consequences of being caught were quite benign: a smashed still and a fine by the sheriff. Everybody in Crawford County knew that the sheriff was not talking to the feds, and the feds were busy down in Kentucky and Tennessee. And Wisconsin was full of law-abiding citizens, and everybody knew that. If a hunter came across a still tucked into the brush, he might smile and pass right by.

They say that opposites attract, and Clara was another sort of person altogether. She was described as a sweet, innocent girl, her father's favorite, said people. Erdman was her first love. She had met a few possible beaus, the term widely used to mean boyfriend, at church socials, a few dances, that sort of occasion. But she never had a steady boyfriend. Erdman, on the other hand, went to many dances but seldom took Clara. She knew that Erdman was seeing and dancing with other young ladies, but she didn't think many wrote letters to him, not the way she did.

When he was away at Gale College, they wrote back and forth, exchanging letters every few days. She treasured the letters from Erdman and read them over and over, sitting by the window looking out on the driveway. Her younger sister, Alice, sometimes peeked over her shoulder. Alice was the snoopy one, their father would later tell reporters.

Clara was a dutiful daughter. She kept close to home, did the chores, milking cows, baking, washing and ironing clothes, working the tobacco crop. She hired out to neighbors as a domestic, as the term was used. Clara was also true to her Norwegian Lutheran faith.

Erdman dated Clara whenever he came home from Gale College. Oddly, he never came into the house, declining each time Chris Olson beckoned him in. Never even walked up the front steps. Chris never talked to his daughter's suitor face to face. Erdman always made excuses not to enter the house and be introduced to Clara's family.

Her father said later that the Erdman always wanted to meet his daughter someplace away from the family home. He had to be content with what Alice told him about the young man. Clara confided in Alice, because they kept each other's secrets.

Clara would go bounding out of the house, hop in Erdman's Ford Roadster, and disappear among the hills and valleys of Crawford County. At times they would sit for hours in his car, talking.

The next spring, in 1926, when Erdman returned from Gale College for the Easter break, the two lovers took long drives in the countryside. Perhaps the springtime air, the apple trees blossoming, the whole countryside greening up beautifully under the warm sun and southern breezes, overtook them. There were several known lover's lanes scattered across the verdant landscape. One of those was a turnoff into the woods known as Battle Ridge, about a mile south of Rising Sun, on Highway 27, called the Black River Road.

The expanse of woods was not large. The Erdman Olson farmstead could be glimpsed through the trees to the east, about a quarter mile away. Other lover's lanes were found along the bluffs of the Mississippi River. The young people of Crawford County knew them all. Cars meant mobility and freedom, perhaps too much freedom, their Norwegian elders would say.

At some point during that vacation, passion gave way to submission and release. There would be talk later, in low voices and whispers. Did Clara know what she was doing? Surely, she knew the consequences of a sexual relationship. She was a farm girl. She knew about cows and bulls, rams and ewes, boars and sows. Her older sisters, Minnie and Emma, had warned Clara, "All boys want is sex. They'll tell you anything, flatter you, but what they want is your body."

More whispers at taverns, quilting bees, church picnics. How many times did she and Erdman have sex? Did he force himself on her? Did she resist, or was she a willing partner?

Did Erdman Olson have access to condoms? Rudolph Valentino was the "great lover" of that era. Valentino played an Arabian sheik in a number of silent movies. Women swooned to his love scenes. When he died at age 31 in August 1926, thousands of women went crazy. Two killed themselves. It was no accident that an image of the sheik was put onto the condom tins of the 1920s.

While premarital sex is age-old, talking about it wasn't. In the 1920s, sex exploded on the scene, partly due to Prohibition, but also because after World War I women had gained the right to vote. An editorial in an August 1920 issue of the *Ladies' Home Journal* stated, "With new social thinking and activities come new social conventions. Most prominently, sex has become far less taboo than it has been previously. Sex is more openly discussed and premarital sex more common. Such activity leads naturally to the promotion of birth control, though it is still widely illegal. The sexual revolution has brought with it changing ideas about women."

By the December 1925 issue of *Harper's Monthly*, Beatrice M. Hinkle would write, "The great movement which is now sweeping over the land, affecting the women of all classes, carries with it something immeasurable, for it is the destroyer of the old mold which for ages has held women bound to instinct."

During the 1920s, traditional notions of proper behavior were challenged. Buoyed by the decade's prosperity, young people threw raucous parties, drank illegal liquor, and danced new, sexually suggestive steps at jazz clubs. One of the symbols of this decade was the flapper, a name given to the fashionable, pleasure-seeking young women of the time. The archetypal flapper look was tomboyish and flamboyant: short bobbed hair; knee-length, fringed skirts; long, draping necklaces; and rolled stockings. Although few women actually fit this image, it was used widely in journalism and advertising to represent the rebelliousness of the period. The traditional bastions of American morality lamented these developments, and especially criticized the new dances and college students' proclivity for drinking and smoking.

Lillian Symes, also writing in *Harper's Monthly*, expressed this view of the radical changes when she stated that feminists' "attempts at economic and social emancipation" have put them in the position of "playing both a man's and a woman's part. ... Instead of achieving freedom, they have achieved the right to carry two burdens, to embrace a new form of servitude." Concerned about the future of the social order, Symes added, "Old values are giving way to what seems a loss of all values."

The whispers, questions, and innuendos about Erdman and Clara would continue for many years. How many times did they have sex? "Well, it only takes once," a few wags would remind others in their company. Did Erdman promise marriage to Clara? The only people that know were the two of them tangled in that car.

Erdman's conduct in other areas of his life, however, indicated that he was hardly ready to settle down. In a newspaper account published after Clara's funeral, the *Winona Republican Herald* reported, "On one occasion, he attacked a student in a quarrel and knocked him out, whereupon other college boys took him in hand. Early this year when a disgraceful performance in one of the dormitories and was reported, Olson is said to have been the leader. His roommate, Grinde, says that Olson had a revolver in his trunk." The paper reported other disturbing incidents as well. "At one time during this fall Olson was said to be a leader in a 'disgraceful performance' at the college in which a dummy was hung from a dormitory window. He had a 22-calibre revolver in his room and at times was known to have fired it into the wall. His room was generally unkempt."

In the same article his rebellious side was exposed: "Early in April, 1926, Erdman and two other students were the leaders of a strike of all students at the college who refused to return to school until the three youths had been reinstated. The students had already left the college and were walking toward the business district of the city when the strike was called off and the boys admitted to school again."

The president of Gale College, K. Lokensgard, said they learned of "indiscreet conduct of Erdman Olson during Easter vacation." The college would not divulge the nature of the conduct. Lokensgard further stated, "On April 18, 1926, when he returned to school, he was given the choice of a formal expulsion, or that of quietly and immediately leaving school. He chose the latter course, and it was noted that his conduct previous to this affair was very unsatisfactory."

Erdman chose to fight his dismissal. In both written and oral appeals, he begged for a new opportunity. The school authorities, believing him to be sincere in his regret of past conduct, and believing he sincerely desired to gain an education, agreed that he could reenter school in September. He was given to understand that he was on probation.

Erdman did not know that his mother had personally visited President Lokensgard in his office at Gale College and begged for her son's reinstatement.

By early May, Clara would have experienced the first signs that she was pregnant. She would have missed her period. Did she have morning sickness around the middle of May? As May was succeeded by June, Clara would have gained further clarity. Yet she told no one, not even her closest sister, Alice.

She was writing letters to her lover, Erdman. He would write back, almost every day. Did she tell him that she was pregnant? Did he stop coming down to Stoney Point Road to see her? Or did those letters contain a promise of marriage?

In the meantime, she had her work to do as a member of the family. Early May was the time Vernon and Crawford County tobacco farmers planted the seedlings into the fields, about one week after the last killing frost. The season had already started well before that. In March, the tiny tobacco seeds were spread over the rich soil placed in long trays formed by 2 x 4 lumber. A tobacco bed was typically 36 inches wide. Fine soil covered the seeds. Many growers went down in the woods and dug stump dirt to enrich the soil. The seedlings were watered with a sprinkling can, then covered by white tobacco cloth, a lightweight, loosely woven cotton fabric.

In frugal Norwegian tradition, this tobacco cloth was reused year after year, cleaned, dried, and rolled up for next year's seedlings. Some of the worn-out cloth was made into curtains for the house, some used for straining milk, draining gristle, bandages, and tea bags. Some tobacco cloth was dyed various colors and made into dresses, blouses, and hats. Brides chose tobacco cloth for wedding veils. It augmented the cloth farmers acquired from feed sacks and seed sacks.

A month after Erdman Olson planted a seed into Clara Olson, the tobacco seedlings were germinating, covered with cloth for 25 days in a greenhouse and watered periodically.

Then the four-inch-tall seedling plants were removed from the bed and planted in the field. The tobacco fields had been already prepared, the soil broken with a plow, fertilized by cow, horse, sheep, and chicken manure, followed by disking and smoothing by a drag.

In early June the planter, pulled by two horses, wended through the field. Three workers were required to plant tobacco. One person drove the team of horses or mules. An attached barrel of water watered the plants. Two farm workers sat on seats low to the ground with a tray of young tobacco plants seated on their lap. A rotating clicking device signaled each person to set a plant into the ground. Clara, riding the planter that spring, had to be wondering about the seed growing inside her.

On a beautiful sunny day, with a light breeze, a few cumulus clouds overhead, crows cawing and an occasional cow bellowing in the distance, Clara Olson didn't know that she had only 100 days to live.

(Top) *A photo of Erdman Olson and his classmates at Gale College in early 1926. Erdman is standing second from the left. The photo is on page 29 of their yearbook called* The Pennant.
(Bottom) *Gale College, in Galesville, Wisconsin, was found in 1854 by George Gale. The Synod of the Norwegian Evangelical Lutheran Church in America purchased the college in 1901. Its buildings included two dormitories, the main building, and a heating building. The main building has been restored by the Old Main Historical & Community Arts Center. Albert Olson sent his eldest son, Erdman Sanford Olson, age 16, to Gale College. His attendance came with a roadster, stylish clothes, and more than sufficient spending money.*

CHAPTER 4

The Dog Days of August

All through June the farm work went on. Shortly after planting, Chris Olson moved through the field with a bucket of tobacco plants, filling in for missing plants. A broomlike stick with a sharp point made an opening in the ground. The plant was inserted into the hole and soil was pushed around it. Stooping hand labor with heat, humidity, flies, and mosquitoes as companions.

The household had many helpful hands. Older boys, Adolph and Bernard, were young, strong, and farming savvy. Clara's young sisters, Alice, Cornelia, and Inga, toiled in the fields and did household chores. Oldest sister, Minnie, now in her middle thirties, was working in La Crosse. Arthur had been hired for electrical work in Milwaukee.

Every few days Clara was called to do domestic house work for the neighbors. When the mother in the household was sick and couldn't cook, Clara was asked to fill in. Or if a neighbor lady was delivering a newborn. Clara answered the call to cook, clean, and do laundry. If the Utica Lutheran Church was hosting an early summer picnic after services on Sunday, Clara helped with cooking, baking, preparing the dishes, serving food, collecting and washing the dishes. She was a dutiful, religious Norwegian girl.

The summer forged into July. The one-row horse-drawn cultivator was pulled through the tobacco field, preventing weeds and loosening the soil to accept rain water. Hoeing around the plants was also needed to cut the weeds and open the soil for moisture.

Chris Olson and his family moved through the fields, topping the tobacco plants, removing the flower heads to prevent cross-pollination and pushing the roots deeper. Seeds were collected from a few healthy plants. A bag was placed over the top of the flower head.

A few days after the flower head was removed, suckers started growing at the base of the leaf. Another trek through the tobacco fields sliced off the suckers on the plants. The suckers used moisture and nutrients, and the grower wanted those to feed the tobacco leaves. Clara and younger sisters Alice, Cornelia, and Inga would take part in combing through the tobacco plots.

The Olson family would head through the fields once again in order to pick off the enemies of a good tobacco harvest. Tobacco pests, such as the tobacco horn worm, can eat an entire leaf in one afternoon. For Clara, there were always the domestic chores of a Wisconsin farm: doing the washing, hanging the wet laundry on the clothes lines outside on the north lawn, and ironing clothes. Cooking was done on a wood-burning stove in a small building or shed close to the house. There was no air conditioning, not even electric fans to cool people.

All the while Clara knew a child was growing inside her. It was her dark secret. What agony did she suffer in those summer months of 1926? Did she make a mistake? Did she give herself to a man, actually a boy of 18, that was not thinking in terms of marriage?

Clara came from stock that was independent and stoic, sons and daughters of Norwegian immigrants, working hard all week and worshiping on Sunday in the Lutheran churches dotting the verdant countryside.

July shifted into August. Hoeing the tobacco fields, topping the flowers, removing the suckers, pulling off pests that can devastate a tobacco plant.

Other young man and women in their late teens and early twenties were attending dances in Seneca and going on church picnics and socials. But not Clara. She sat in her upstairs room, reading and rereading the letters from her lover, Erdman Olson.

About August 1, after 17 weeks of pregnancy, Clara felt her unborn baby move inside her. In the company of her family, she was quiet, even a bit remote and morose. She quietly struggled on. Hope against hope, for a marriage, for a husband, for a family, for domestic bliss. What had happened wasn't so bad. It was the way her own parents had become married, and that had turned out well.

By August 17, Clara was desperate and could wait no longer. She would soon start to show her pregnancy and had secretly purchased or borrowed a maternity corset. Clara sat at a small desk in her room, light coming in the south window. On gold-edged stationery paper, using blue-black ink, Clara penned a letter to Albert and Anna Olson, telling them that she was beyond four months pregnant.

> Dear Mr. and Mrs. Albert Olson—I know you folks will be surprised to hear from me and what I have to say. Understand I am a good friend to your Erdman and am sorry to say that we are in a pinch and have to get married—if God is willing and you folks are willing to help us. I wrote Erdman a letter some time ago to come down and marry me because I do not want to get him in trouble, and I don't want my parents to know, and I hope you folks will help us before my folks find out what has come.
>
> Please be good to Erdman. I know he never meant to leave me. It is only four-and-one-half months left now until I will be expecting. So I hope Erdman and I can get married this month and make our lives worthwhile. I am closing with love, and God's blessing, and I hope to hear from you and see Erdman soon.

Since the closing of the Rising Sun Post Office some 20 years earlier, the mail went to Ferryville, down over the bluffs along the Mississippi River. The Albert Olsons received Clara's letter two days later, on August 19. The letter was picked up from the mailbox at the end of their long gravel driveway. Albert and Anna Olson were appraised that their son was the father of a child that was to be born shortly after Christmas.

The letter "hit the fan," so to speak. Erdman's parents showed the letter to their son. Erdman shrugged it off. In later testimony Albert Olson stated that Erdman "seemed surprised" when told the contents of the letter. He should not have been. Clara's letters to her lover explained that she was "in a family way."

Albert Olson ordered his son to go get the girl and bring her to their home. "Have her submit to an examination," the parents demanded. "I'd never seen the girl," Albert Olson said later in testimony. "I didn't know anything about her. I told Erdman to get a doctor to examine the girl and get the truth."

"Tell her to come see us," said Erdman's mother.

Clara refused. Perhaps she knew the intent of the Olson family was to procure an abortion. In those days, it was termed an "illegal operation."

Erdman told his parents: "She got her dates mixed." He was telling his parents that Clara must be dating other young men, hence her pregnancy was not of his doing. They believed him. The parents' thinking went along these lines: Clara got herself in a mess. She needed a husband. She was probably after Erdman's inheritance. It was a trap. She had enticed him. After all, she was four years older than Erdman. "He was no more than a child," Erdman's mother said later. "He is a boy not fully grown yet."

Yet unknown to his parents, Erdman had a darker side that set him apart from other young men. He carried a revolver to these dances and would slyly flash it to his friends. This was in keeping with the bootlegging ethos of the day.

Prohibition brought an unprecedented wave of lawlessness. Bootlegging—the manufacture, transportation, and selling of illegal booze—became a major industry in the United States. Speakeasies, political bribery, bathtub gin, and running booze into the United States from Canada and Mexico all became part of the Prohibition landscape. Rival gangs shot up major cities. The streets of New York were filled with shootouts between rival gangs run by the likes of Lucky Luciano, Dutch Schultz, and Legs Diamond. In Chicago, gang shootouts flared during the "Beer Wars" from 1922 to 1926, when mobsters killed more than 300 of their own and police officers killed another 160. All of this murderous activity was widely reported in newspapers at the time.

A young man growing up on a tobacco farm would never encounter such a foe. Certainly, he did not need a weapon for self-defense. Crawford County was devoid of big city gangs. Yet toting a pistol was in keeping with Erdman's character: toughness, dominance, and a willingness to resort to violence to get his way.

There is little question that he was influenced by the culture of bootlegging. Many believed that gangsters carried around guns in violin cases, because the Thompson submachine gun, affectionately referred to as a "Chicago typewriter," was carried in a case remarkably similar in shape to a violin case. This notion made its way onto the screen of the movie theatres, such as the ones Erdman patronized in Viroqua, La Crosse, and Prairie du Chien.

In fact, gangsters carried their "hardware" in newspapers. Newspapers in the 1920s were much larger than they are today, almost twice the size. Any weapon, handgun, rifle, or machine gun, could be easily concealed in a rolled-up newspaper. Tellingly, Erdman would later mail his pistol home to his parents in a rolled-up newspaper.

As daring as he was at night, however, he still was the son of a tobacco farmer. Normal life went on in the hill country through the long, hot dog days of summer. Farmers were threshing oats, putting up second crop hay, and tending to the tobacco crop. They feared the summer storms that blew across Crawford County. Lightning could kill cows seeking shelter in groves of trees. Lightning ignited barns, setting back decades of hard work. Hail stripped the leaves off tobacco plants and corn stalks. Devastating winds could flatten oats and wheat fields. The Norwegian clergy invoked prayer and asked God to spare them any calamities.

The early morning fog drifted over the Kickapoo and Mississippi River bottoms, ravines, and low valleys. The fog was burned off by the blazing sun, come nine or ten o'clock in the morning.

Northern Crawford County was populated by poor but honest farmers, mostly Norwegian, some Irish, and some German. Many were first generation, and conversations at churches and social gatherings rang of the language of the old country.

The night life continued for the young people. They worked hard but played hard. There were dances at Seneca, always with live music, well attended, continuing past midnight, even on weekday nights. Eighteen-year-old Erdman Olson danced, drank, and carried on with the young ladies of Rising Sun, Mt. Sterling, and Seneca. The Norwegian clergy did not look kindly on "this foolishness." Their sermons in the Lutheran churches were laced with condemnation of the "dancing, drinking, and carrying-on" by the young people. Norwegian elders nodded in agreement. "These young folks are going to hell in a handbasket," an older woman was heard to say.

Clara Olson continued to sit in the big white farmhouse out on Stony Point Road. She worked by day and read Erdman's letters over and over. She did not attend any dances. Erdman did not take her. Pregnancy was a great shame even in the roaring twenties. And Clara could not hide the life she was carrying any longer.

From the date Clara wrote her pleading letter to Erdman's parents, August 17, 1926, she has 23 days to live.

THE WARSAW UNION

WORLD'S NEWS BY ASSOCIATED PRESS

WARSAW, INDIANA, MONDAY, DECEMBER 6, 1926

CLARA OLSON APPEALED TO FATHER OF LOVER

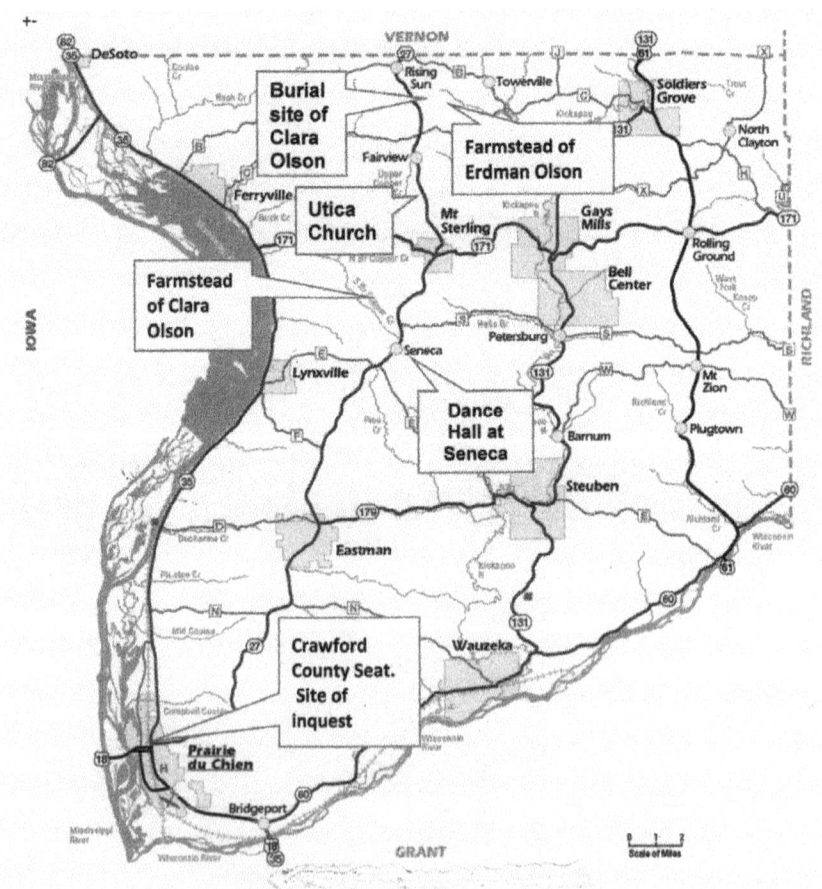

Map of sites of the tragic Clara Olson story in Crawford County, Wisconsin.

CHAPTER 5

Erdman Olson Mulls His Options

What was going on in the mind of the young father-to-be? Surely, he saw himself in a mess, trapped in a situation of his own making. His lover, Clara, was about to give birth to his child in less than five months. Who did he blame more, himself or Clara?"

Erdman was mulling over his options as he went about the summer tasks of tending to the tobacco crop, milking cows, mending fences, repairing machinery, and getting the tobacco shed ready for harvest. He could not totally deny responsibility. Clara had letters from him in which he acknowledged his culpability, and yes, promised her marriage.

Denial would not work. He had owned up to his sexual deeds in those letters. Clara had these letters, and he knew it. He was ensnared in a web of deceit of his own making. He realized he could not blame some other suitor. Erdman was the only boyfriend that Clara ever had. Oh, she had gone out with other fellows, including the Albert Olson hired hand, Edwin Knutson. He drove her home one time. But that was just to a church social or to a dance. Ed Knutson transporting Clara home one evening could hardly be construed as a date. Erdman Olson was trapped, and he knew it.

Did Erdman really love Clara, or did he see her as a release for his sexual urges? Marriage might not be out of the question. He could marry the girl, have the baby, and perhaps divorce down the road. Maybe he could be content with a "woman on the side," an expression used for infidelity.

Erdman Olson was pondering all his options. The pending decision was weighing heavily on his mind as he went about his daily routines. It took him 21 days to decide. No marriage. There would be no "shotgun wedding." That was the colloquial term used for a wedding that was arranged to avoid embarrassment due to an unplanned pregnancy rather than stemming from the wishes of the participants. The father of the daughter that had premarital sex would resort to using coercion, such as threatening with a shotgun, to ensure that the young male lover would follow through with the wedding. Such a wedding would restore the social honor of the mother and ensure that the child would be raised by both parents.

Erdman would not be snared into such an onerous union with Clara. He was mulling over a way out of his problem. He was thinking deep, dark, forbidding thoughts. If there was no Clara, there was no problem. If Clara disappears, my problems disappear, he was thinking.

He might have been thinking of the daring shown by Nathan Leopold Jr. and Richard Albert Loeb, usually referred to collectively as Leopold and Loeb. They were two wealthy students at the University of Chicago who in May 1924 kidnapped and murdered 14-year-old Robert Franks. They committed the murder, widely characterized at the time as "the crime of the century" as a demonstration of their perceived intellectual superiority, which, they thought, rendered them capable of carrying out a perfect crime and absolved them of responsibility for their actions.

After the two men were arrested, Loeb's parents retained Clarence Darrow as counsel for their defense. Darrow's 12-hour-long summation at their sentencing hearing is noted for its influential criticism of capital punishment as retributive rather than transformative justice. Nonetheless, both of them were sentenced to life imprisonment, plus 99 years (Wikipedia).

Regardless of any precedents, the die was cast. The time for pondering were over. It was time for action. One night in early September, Erdman Olson sat at the kitchen table of his parents' house and wrote a letter in pencil. The letter would seal the fate of both young lovers. He would lure Clara Olson to her death.

Ferryville, Wis Sept 6, 1926

Dear Friend:

I suppose you think me awfully neglectful, but I haven't. I have been to the hospital for a while, had a couple of operations. I have decided the time for us is right to show action. Of course, we'll have to disappear you know so I thought we could get the ceremony over with and then come back in a week or so and let them know if they don't know. You'll have to coax your brother to take you down to Seneca to the dance Sept. 9th and I will get you there. Then we then go to Hendrum, Minnesota, which is the same as Winona. Do not take any more clothes than what you wear as taking more will cause suspicion and try to get as much cash as possible as that is necessary if we wish to make a pleasant trip out of it. I have some myself of course.

I will be at Seneca between 9 and 10 o'clock and when you see me, leave the hall alone and walk up the street until I find you and remember that everything is on the Q.T. (quiet), also write a note and leave some place where it can be found in a day or so and say that you are going away for a while but not to worry as you'll be back someday but don't mention why you were going nor mention my name. If you can't come to the dance, sneak out of the house about 12:30 and come towards the road. If I am not there keep on going until I meet you. Don't let anyone see you. Please destroy this letter and all my other letters and act hard towards me to your folks.

Do as I have asked you to do and everything will be OK. If you don't your chance might be shot and I might make a scarce hubby, so if you wish to avoid the disgrace do as I say and keep mum.

See you on the 9th.

As ever.

As usual.

P.S.—Remember, do as I say, and destroy all letters.

On September 9, Clara received the above long letter from Erdman. Bernard brought it in from the mailbox along the Stoney Point road. The time was 2 PM. Clara Olson had no idea that she would be dead in 10 hours.

THE MILWAUKEE JOURNAL

Find Letters on Slain Girl's Body

Ice at Soo May Hold Boats All Winter

Big Snow Sends Hunters Scurrying Southward in Cars

Clara Olson Was Killed by Blow Behind Her Ear

Chris and Dina Olson raised ten children in this grand and rambling 2-story house on Stoney Point Road, a few miles north of Seneca.

CHAPTER 6

A Fateful Day

To understand the relief Clara Olson felt, it is necessary to regard the term "illegitimate" the way people did in the 1920s. It designated an unmarried mother, sometimes father, and their child. The unlucky child was sometimes viewed by polite society as "deviant," and the term "bastard" was freely heard.

An unmarried girl was sent to a special hospital or an isolated maternity home to have her baby. Her shame was hidden behind closed doors. The young mother was not allowed to see her newborn baby, let alone hold the child in her arms. In most cases, the baby was put up for adoption promptly. Some were taken in by dangerous "baby farms" and later sold to parents wanting to adopt.

In the 1920s the belief was widespread that children born out of wedlock presented significant social and public health problems. Illegitimacy was believed to be a factor in mental deficiency, disease, and antisocial behavior. Feeble-minded children were more likely to be borne by unmarried women because illegitimate pregnancies were byproducts of retardation, insanity, and epilepsy.

Leading psychoanalysis of the time, Marion Kenworthy, Jessie Taft, and Viola Bernard, encouraged social workers to consider nonmarital pregnancies as expressions of neurosis.

Girls and women who had sex before or outside of marriage got pregnant on purpose, whether they knew it or not, according to their Freudian worldview.

The social stigma unfairly fell onto the woman. Her partner often escaped the responsibility, blame, shame, and humiliation. Many times he escaped financial accountability as well. Even so, if the young man "did the right thing" and married his lover, there was little or no stigma involved.

Clara Olson had heard these stories. Marriage to Erdman was so dear to her. She wanted to believe that her Erdman would take the honorable course.

Clara received Erdman's letter at two o'clock in the afternoon on Thursday, September 9. Her spirits were lifted. At last, Erdman was going to do what she had pleaded with him to do. His letter to Clara was postmarked September 8 from Ferryville, down along the Mississippi River. Her sister Alice watched her open it. Clara read the penciled folded pages.

Clara read the letter over and over while Alice tried to read over her shoulder. Clara had her instructions on what to do. This much Alice realized because a flurry of activity followed.

Clara folded the letter into tight squares, then slipped it into her bodice. She went into the parlor, took down a geography book from the shelf, and began paging through it, checking the index several times. Alice asked Clara what she was looking for. "Oh, a place," she said.

She couldn't find Hendrum, Minnesota, which is east of Fargo, North Dakota, 400 miles away on the Red River, which divides Minnesota and North Dakota.

Clara searched further in the family geography book. She understood that "we will go to Hendrum, which is the same as Winona," was essentially a proposal of marriage. In 1926, young people in Wisconsin had to apply for a wedding license and then wait seven days, during which time the announcement was made public, and the couple had a physical examination. There was no such law in Minnesota. A couple could obtain a marriage license and get married on the same day. It was quite common for couples in Crawford County to go cross the Mississippi River to Winona to get hitched.

She climbed the stairs to her room. She took all her letters from Erdman, which she had stuffed in a book. She always hid the envelopes under the rug. Alice came up to watch. Clara burned all her letters, keeping back only two. One was in pencil, the other in ink. She could not bear to part with those. She raised the hob and threw the letters into the wood-burning stove. Now smiling, now musing with regret over some phrase that had struck a chord, Clara had dreams and plans for a wonderful life ahead.

Alice observed Clara fiddling with the lamp in the window of her second-floor bedroom. She drew up a blind three times, positioning it so the shade could be used to make a crude flashing signal once night fell.

In the late afternoon, Chris and daughter Clara drove to Seneca. While he most likely was shopping for farm supplies, she bought clothes for her upcoming escape. The town served the farming countryside. Nelius Tollefson ran a pool hall. Jack (Pepper) Keyes was a very busy blacksmith. John Coughlin operated a garage and sold new cars. John Fitzgibbon had a farm in the village limits. The Finley family pastured cows behind their house. Clara bought new dresses, new shoes, and other clothes.

When they returned home, she helped with the evening milking. She fed and watered the chickens. At supper, she sat pale and silent. All the while Alice wondered what thoughts must be going through her mind.

***

Seven miles north of the Chris Olson farm was the site of another flurry of activity. Erdman Olson had loaded his Ford Roadster with pick, shovel, ax, and post hole digger. Out of the driveway, north on Highway 27 several hundred yards away was a logging road. He turned right and drove into the woods about 300 feet. The site was known as Battle Ridge. The hill had received its name in Indian days. It was here in 1832 that

Black Hawk and his warriors made one of their last stands to save the Kickapoo Valley from the white men.

Tools in hand, Erdman turned over several shovels of soil. It was tough going with the ground laced with roots of nearby trees. Realizing he had picked the wrong spot, he dragged the dirt back into the started grave, and moved to one that was more promising.

Erdman dug, shovelful after shovelful. The roots he encountered needed cutting. He was calculating, about six feet long and maybe about three feet deep and three feet wide. That should be more than enough. Soon he was perspiring. On that late summer day, the temperature reached a high of 74, typical for the hill country of southwest Wisconsin.

After Erdman had been at the task for over an hour, he must have started to worry. Any more time might raise suspicions with his folks, Albert and Anna, and with the hired man, Edwin Knutson. He finished his gruesome task by about three o'clock.

***

At the Chris Olson farmstead, Clara baked cookies, then helped prepare supper. When chores and meal were finished, she retreated to her upstairs room, sat at a small desk table, and wrote a note for her parents.

> Dear folks;
>
> I know you all will be surprised to find me gone, as I am leaving this evening. I will have to go tonight. Please do not worry about me as I will not be gone very long. If anyone asks about me tell them that I have gone to La Crosse. Again, I must tell you do not worry about me as I am taken good care of and will be back soon. Don't take it too seriously as it will mean nothing—only a little surprise. I will be back soon from my trip.

Clara placed the note under a lamp, with just a corner sticking out. She lay in bed but dared not sleep.

How could the thoughts of the future of two individuals be so diametrically opposed? Clara envisioned a future with marriage, birth of her child, a home, and domestic bliss. Erdman had murder on his agenda, the solution to his problem with his hick girlfriend.

Clara Olson has 3 hours to live.

(Top) *View of Battle Ridge from the Albert Olson farm.*
(Bottom) *Burial site among the black and red oaks on Battle Ridge. The grave was 30 feet from an old logging road.*

CHAPTER 7

Murder in the Hill Country

Seneca held Thursday night dances at the pool hall, dance hall, and hotel owned by Grace Tollefson. People referred to it as Neil's hall. That Thursday night a band from Lansing Iowa, was playing in the dance hall on the second floor.

At 11:00 Erdman Olson drove past the general store. A stranger was seated in the passenger seat of his Ford Roadster. Merle Murray, a farm lad from Mt. Sterling, was standing out in front. Erdman asked Murray, "Do you want some booze?" "Yes," was the reply, and the three of them went around to the back and passed around a bottle. While Merle bought another bottle from Erdman, the stranger retreated to the car and remained there.

The two young men walked into the pool hall, stayed a few minutes, engaged in a few conversations, and then took the stairs to the second-floor dance hall. They talked for a few minutes with the owner of a hotel in Mt. Sterling, Park Morris.

Erdman proceeded to dance the foxtrot with Marie Anderson and her cousin Christine Anderson. Marie was a good friend of Clara Olson's younger sister, Alice. As Erdman was dancing, Park Morris and Merle Murray sauntered over to the window and spotted Erdman's Roadster and the stranger sitting on the passenger side. In later testimony at the inquest,

Marie Anderson would recall that Erdman was drunk. Christine said, "He couldn't keep step."

Of course, Erdman Olson had been drinking. He was filling up with liquid courage. He had a foul deed to carry out.

Merle Murray and Park Morris walked Erdman out to his car. Merle and Park got a look at the stranger. It was dark, but they saw him there. Erdman entered his car and drove away with the stranger, never to be identified, leaving the dance hall at 11:35 PM. He sped away into the mist of the evening in the direction of Stony Point. He had an appointment to keep.

Out on Stoney Point Road, in his rambling farmhouse, Chris Olson was restless. He later recalls the night. "It was about five minutes to twelve when I blew out the light," he said. "Clara went out just a couple of minutes after I went to bed. Then I seen a car. I didn't see no person. I looked through my front door and I seen him turn around this way ..."

Chris dozed off. When he woke up, he turned to his wife. "Clara didn't come back, did she?"

"Yes, I think she did," replied Dina.

Both fell asleep. He said later he had a dream. The gist of it went like this: "I walked past Clara's room and looked in. Her bed was empty. I woke up frightened. I told Dina to go see about Clara. She did. Clara's bed was empty."

Clara had climbed in the Ford Roadster, and she and Erdman were off. It was slightly past midnight. Erdman reached Highway 27, turned left, and motored toward Mt. Sterling. It is not hard to imagine that Clara asked Erdman about their elopement and honeymoon destination. They were going to Hendrum, Minnesota, or so he stated in his letter of instructions to her. Clara had searched the family atlas book for such a town but found nothing.

Where did Erdman come up with the name Hendrum, Minnesota? The Albert Olson family did have relatives out in the Dakotas. Laid out in 1881, Hendrum had been named after a place in Norway.

Did she ask him about it? Most likely, Clara didn't really care where she was headed. She was in the capable care of her lover and soon-to-be husband and father. Her fears and anxieties had vanished. Clara was one happy young woman.

One can only speculate about the conversation during that ten-mile drive. Did they talk about their wedding or where they would spend the first night? After all, it was getting on toward midnight. Did Clara ask Erdman where they would stop for the evening? Perhaps Viroqua? They were headed that way. Maybe La Crosse? Bigger city, a good selection of hotels, and only an hour's drive time. Erdman slowed his Roadster slightly as they passed through the village of Mt. Sterling. Everyone was asleep. Then they headed northward toward Viroqua.

Did they discuss where they would get married? Minister or justice of the peace or a judge in a distant town? Did Erdman ask Clara what she had brought with her? He saw her tote along a bag or satchel or box. How much money did she bring? The young couple passed the Utica Norwegian Lutheran Church, established in 1871, and site of her confirmation a few years earlier. That was Clara's family church. Church services every Sunday with her family. Funerals, picnics, weddings; she'd attended them all, worked in the kitchen in the undercroft. Took her turn cleaning the aisles. A dutiful Norwegian lass, a good daughter, faithful Lutheran.

Where would they live when they returned? How would they make a living? Would his and her parents give them a starter house, or land, cattle or money? Would they live in Galesville while he continued his studies at Gale College? They passed the small settlement of Fairview. The countryside was dark except for a few farms sporting dim kerosene lamps.

Did either of them raise the question of the pending birth of their baby? Both knew that their baby was due just past Christmas.

Or perhaps they did not talk at all. During this 20-minute journey, Clara was feeling relief, justification for her patience, the happiest she had ever been in her life. Her older sisters, Minnie and Emma, were unmarried and edging toward spinsterhood. Whereas Clara had snagged a big fish. Young, handsome, virile, college-educated, and of good Norwegian stock.

And it sure didn't hurt at all to be wealthy. There was nothing but sunshine and brightness in her future.

The man in charge, the driver of his own Ford Roadster, had a completely different frame of mind. Erdman Olson, an 18-year-old college boy, had decided on murder. He saw his lover's death as the only way out of an entanglement of his own making. He was far too young to get married, have a family, and settle down. Besides, he was looking more to a business career, not tobacco farming. He could do better than that.

They approached the turnoff road to his own farm, a farm on which he was born and raised for 18 years. The car passed the Tully school, which he had attended for his primary grade school education. In several hundred yards, Erdman slowed the car and turned onto a logging road. What reason or excuse did he give Clara for leaving the main highway? Did he need a quick bathroom break? Did he ask her to make love to him before they eloped? Did he tell her that he had his own suitcase of clothes stashed in the woods?

Erdman maneuvered the car along slight curves here and there until he reached the trees a good ways off the main road. The vehicle came to a stop. The freshly dug grave remained hidden in the dark.

The moon that night was in the waxing crescent phase. It had come up an hour after the sun and trailed the sun across the sky. When the sun set, the moon would have remained in view on the western horizon for a while. But now, at midnight, the moon was well gone, well below the western skyline. The night was pitch black, perfect for killing.

Breezes caused the rustling of the leaves. Night sounds, owls, birds, cows in the pastures of distant farms. The air had cooled to 50 degrees, requiring a jacket or sweater.

Authorities later speculated what happened next. Clara might have been sitting in the car when he struck her. But most likely, she got out of the car, and Erdman picked up a steel pipe or small hammer from the back of the Ford and approached Clara from behind.

Erdman swung the weapon with a mighty force, and Clara crumpled to the ground with a moan. The massive trauma caused almost instant death. The autopsy would later confirm that a triangular section of the left rear side of Clara's skull was caved in. Later, her father found out in conversation with Seneca lads that Erdman shot pool left-handed.

Erdman dragged Clara's body to the shallow grave that he had dug hours earlier. It was 30 feet slightly downhill from the logging road. Even in early September, Erdman could see, through the trees, the dim lights from his own farm buildings.

Erdman dumped Clara in the Battle Ridge soil, face down. Quickly he shoveled in the fresh dirt, filling in the tomb of his own creation. Yet he discovered the soil piled up less than one foot over the highest part of Clara's body. When all the dirt was filled in, Erdman stomped the loose soil, making it more compact. No need to leave a telltale depression as the elements will compact the grave over time. A final covering of loose twigs, leaves, and forest material made the grave blend in with the forest floor.

Erdman stood erect and looked over his handiwork. One more task: get rid of the satchel that Clara brought with her. He couldn't take it back to his house.

Erdman turned the car around and headed west to the main road. In another few minutes he turned left onto the long driveway to his farm.

Albert Olson was awake when Erdman came home that night. The chime clock in the parlor struck one o'clock. Erdman walked into the kitchen, turned on the radio, made himself a sandwich, eating while looking through a mail order catalog. He then went to bed.

Clara Olson's dreams had ended in tragedy and death. Now she was merely a crime victim waiting to be discovered. When the sun rose on the eastern horizon, Clara would be dead and buried for seven hours.

$2,500.00 REWARD
Wanted for Murder

A Reward of $2,500.00 will be paid by the undersigned Sheriff of Crawford County, Wisconsin, for the apprehension and delivery to the proper officers of Crawford County, Wis., of Erdman Sanford Olson, wanted for the murder of Clara Olson on September 10th, 1926.

DESCRIPTION
of
Erdman Sanford Olson

AGE:—18 years.

WEIGHT:—About 160 pounds.

HEIGHT:—5 feet, 7½ inches.

HAIR:—Dark brown and combed straight back, sometimes parted in the middle.

EYES:—Blue and has a habit of continually blinking. The eyes turn outward slightly (opposite to cross-eyed).

COMPLEXION:—Light.

NATIONALITY:—Native born—Norwegian descent.

Was a student at Gale College, Galesville, Wisconsin, from which he disappeared September 27th.

Recently had a nasal operation and also had both tonsils removed and two teeth extracted.

Has a habit of standing first on one foot and then the other.

Arrest, hold and wire collect.

Will extradite from any place.

H. W. SHERWOOD, Sheriff, Crawford County, Wis.
P. O. Address, Prairie du Chien, Wisconsin

Wanted poster for Erdman Olson

CHAPTER 8

The Morning After

What attributes of Erdman Olson's personality would compel him to murder his lover with a club on a lonely roadside? While the first impulse is to consider him a psychopath, he fits more within the clinical definitions of a sociopath. Matching up his attributes with psychological literature yields some interesting results.

First, sociopaths are defined as charming. They have high charisma, and people want to be around them. They appear to be worldly, savvy, and often have a strong sex appeal. Erdman fits in that category. Clara Olson was smitten by his charm, good looks, education, and wealth.

Sociopaths are spontaneous and intense. They tend to behave erratically and feel unbound by social norms. Their behavior may seem at times to be irrational and risky. Erdman seems to fit in this category. He would flash a revolver at dances and kept a pistol in his locker at Gale College, an institution for training ministers. Friends and acquaintances could count on Erdman to supply outlawed liquor.

Sociopaths are master wordsmiths who can wax poetic. Clara's sister, Alice, told reporters that Clara would repeat to her some of the Erdman's rhetoric. Clara was taken in, Alice said, by Erdman's suave lines.

Sociopaths are not capable of feeling shame, guilt, or remorse. This allows them to betray people without giving it a second thought. They pursue any action that serves their own self-interest, even if it does serious harm to others. How else to explain Erdman's carefully planning Clara's murder? Of cold-bloodedly writing a note to lure her out, digging a grave beforehand, conversing with her on the drive to Battle Ridge on the pretense of a forthcoming wedding, clubbing her to death, calmly enjoying a snack and listening to the radio at his house, and then shamelessly lying to her brother the next morning? These actions indicate a person who has no empathy for anyone else.

A sociopath, such as Erdman Olson, is not capable of love. They are entirely self-serving. They may feign love, indeed promise marriage and a family. Sex and love are not the same, however. Self-gratifying sex Erdman could do, but not love. In his letters to Clara, he promised marriage, but it was an outrageous lie. He was not about to marry "that hick girl who is in love with me."

Some of these traits would emerge the morning after the murder. Friday, September 10, 1926, dawned with cool temperatures and another threat of rain. The tobacco harvest was nearly completed, with just two acres left standing on the Chris Olson farm. While it was still dark, Chris climbed the creaking wooden stairs leading to the upstairs bedrooms. There was no reply from Clara's room after he rapped lightly on the closed door. Slowly cracking it open, the father peered inside. Clara was missing from her room. The bed had not been slept in. Looking more closely, he spied a corner of Clara's note tucked under the lamp by the window. Chris read it and started trembling.

He woke up his sons, Adolph and Bernard, as he cried out, "Clara is missing." He told them about the car he saw out the window around midnight. Together, they took a lantern and went out to the road. Sure enough, they found tire tracks. Light rains made quite distinctive tracks. One tire in particular had been patched. The tracks led north, toward Erdman Olson's home.

While Adolph returned to the farmstead to start the morning chores and milking, Chris sent Clara's older brother, Bernard, to the farm of Albert Olson, just south of Rising Sun, to inquire after Clara. It was a 15- to 20-minute drive.

Bernard kept in mind the tire print where a car had turned. He had noted the distinctive pattern and observed that three of the tires matched but one didn't. Soon, as Bernard approached the Albert Olson farm buildings, he noted the tire prints along the long driveway at several places.

Bernard had come to the homestead without any definite idea that it was the college boy's Ford Roadster that had turned in the driveway. But he noted the tire treads leading into the farm were the same as those he had seen in the lane on his own father's farm.

It was barely dawn, first light showing in the east, when Bernard knocked on the farmhouse door. Erdman's mother, Anna, later said it was six o'clock. She was cooking breakfast while Albert and the hired hand, Edwin Knutson, were milking cows.

"Well, good morning," said Bernard to Mrs. Olson. She nodded. "Pretty cold this morning," he said.

"Yes, it is," Mrs. Olson responded

"I'm here to see Erdman."

"He's asleep, but I'll see."

Several minutes passed and Erdman came into the kitchen and sat at the family table. "You were up pretty late," said Bernard.

"Yes," Erdman said.

Alice had told her father about Erdman's letter to Clara. Bernard and Adolph knew about it, too, and he brought that subject up next.

"You wrote a letter to Clara the other day?"

"Yes," replied Erdman. He wasn't quite awake.

Bernard pushed, "Where is Clara?"

Erdman retorted, "I don't know. Why?"

"You do know," said Bernard. "It was your car that was in our lane last night. The tire treads are the same."

Erdman quickly changed his story. "Oh, all right, then," he answered. "I took her to Viroqua and gave her fifty dollars."

Bernard pressed, "How is it then that the tire treads show that you drove into your lane here coming from the south when Viroqua is north?" Bernard had noted this fact.

"That's easy," replied the college student. "I told the folks I was going to the dance at Seneca, so when I came back from Viroqua, I went south on the highway and turned around so that it would appear that I was just coming from Seneca when I drove into the driveway here." Another lie, and Erdman was digging a deeper hole.

Erdman told Bernard where he could find the tire treads in the ditch on the highway, showing the place when the turn was made.

Bernard pressed again, "Last night you came after her and I came to know where she went."

Erdman didn't answer. His mother handed him a cup of coffee. He denied seeing Clara. He looked out the window. "I didn't come after her."

Bernard told him about the tire tracks on the road. "Those were your tires, all right."

Yet, Erdman protested, he didn't have a patch on one of his tires. He pulled on his boot and led Bernard outside. The tires on the Roadster were all new.

Bernard was unconvinced, and he and Erdman got into a shouting match on the front lawn. It was overheard by Erdman's mother. "It must have been somebody else," Erdman said.

As they came back inside, Erdman's mother asked what the commotion was about. Bernard explained about his missing sister. Mrs. Olson led Bernard through all the rooms in the house. "So you can be sure your sister's not here."

When Albert Olson came out of the barn, he also talked with Bernard. Later, Albert would testify that Bernard told him he was looking for his sister but that he didn't have a search warrant. He had tracked the car from their gate out to Highway 27 and that the car that turned around had an odd tire.

Not gaining any satisfaction, Bernard drove off. At the end of the driveway, he traced the tracks where Erdman had claimed to have turned around. It was very evident, he would later tell investigator Captain Sullivan, that the car had been pulled off to the side of the road, but a complete turn had not been made.

Bernard went home and told his father what Erdman had said. Clara's family didn't believe a word of it, since all of them knew the only reason Clara would leave the house at midnight was to go meet her boyfriend. They began to make inquiries. News that Clara Olson was missing quickly spread through the close-knit Norwegian community. Most believed that Clara would return home by Christmastime with a baby and no husband, a girl in disgrace. That was the story being put out by the Albert Olson family. The Chris Olson family did get wind of these rumors, but they chose to ignore them.

In any case, Erdman would not be around long to hear about them. As any detective knows, there is no such thing as a coincidence when a crime has been committed, and it is telling that Erdman chose a night so close to his departure for college for the fall semester. It is possible that Clara, also aware of his imminent departure, pressed him. But the timing was very convenient if he wanted to avoid a lot of questions about what happened.

Whatever was the case, Albert, Erdman, his 11-year-old brother Arvid, and hired hand Edwin Knutson had only that weekend to bring in the tobacco before Erdman took off for Gale College. Erdman worked all day Friday, with the others cutting tobacco, tying it, and hanging it in the tobacco shed. The foursome worked all the next day, Saturday, and part of Sunday.

That evening, Erdman went back to Gale College in Galesville, driven by Ed Knutson. Almost as soon as they left home, the car passed by the fateful wooded knoll. Did Erdman look up into that stand of black and red oaks? What thoughts were going through his mind?

That very day Clara Dorthea Olson would have celebrated her 22nd birthday. Instead, she had been murdered by her lover. She, along with her unborn baby girl, lay facedown in a shallow grave atop Battle Ridge.

Chris Olson waited two weeks from the morning of September 10. "If Clara was alive, she would have written me. She was not afraid of me, no matter what was wrong," he would later tell authorities and reporters.

Worry and fear had crept into the household of Chris and Dina Olson. Where was their daughter? If Erdman and Clara had eloped to get married, they would have returned by now. Finally, they could wait no longer.

On Friday, September 24, Chris and Dina went to visit Albert Olson and his wife Anna. The two Olson families had never met. They attended different Norwegian Lutheran churches and lived in different communities. Albert Olson was not home, but Anna was working in the kitchen. After some pleasantries, Chris Olson asked Anna Olson about their daughter Clara.

Anna broke the news about Clara's pregnancy. "I'll remember what she said as long as I live," Chris said later. "She said, don't worry, it would be just like a lot of other girls. Clara will be home after New Year's with a kid and no man. ... That was the first we knew anything about it."

The news hit Chris and Dina hard. It was like a bolt of lightning out of the blue sky. Clara was between five and six months pregnant, but her parents hadn't noticed. It was a shock and disappointment. It would have been their first grandchild.

Further investigation of the disappearance would not have happened without Chris Olson. The devoted father would not let this pass. He would find his daughter Clara. She was his favorite, it was said by a few.

Years of toil in the tobacco fields, logging, milking cows, and pulling out stumps to clear the land had taken its toll. Proud Norwegian patriarch of a large family, Chris appeared older than his 60 years. He stooped slightly, walked slowly, and was hesitant on steps and stairs. Chris exhibited a kindly face, with rumbled hair, pale blue eyes, and rough hands.

He would find his daughter, he told anyone who would listen, but most of them believed, as Anna Olson professed, that Clara was away somewhere waiting for her child to be born. Chris Olson, though, knew something wasn't right. She wouldn't let her family wait for so long without some word. He even had dreams that Clara was dead, he later told reporters.

It was a somber couple that bade goodbye to Anna Olson. They returned to their car and started down the long driveway on out to Highway 27. Little did they know that their Clara was only a few hundreds of yards away, lying beneath a scant foot of soil.

(Top) *Chris Olson, center, is comforted by his children Alice, left, and Bernard Olson on Dec. 6, 1926, while waiting to be called to the stand at the Prairie du Chien inquest into his daughter Clara's slaying.*
(Bottom) *The family of Clara Olson: sisters Emma, 28, from left, Inga, 13, Alice, 19, Cornelia, 16, and Minnie, 34. Clara's parents, Dina Olson and Chris Olson, sit with District Attorney J.S. Earl in December 1926.*

CHAPTER 9

Clara Is Missing

On Sunday, September 26, 1926, Chris asked Oliver and Andrew Helgerson from Mt. Sterling to drive him to Galesville to see Erdman. It's a journey of two hours, about 80 miles, motoring first to La Crosse and heading north to Galesville.

Erdman had been on his best behavior since returning to college. In a later article, the *Winona Republican Herald* found that his classmates described him as a "polished smiling youth, full of life, and of a wholesome appearance, who greeted and ushered the guests from building to building last September, when the 25th anniversary of the school was celebrated."

The newspaper article went on to portray the positive side of the charming young killer. "The clever, winning Erdman Olson who played important roles in school plays, who sang in the choir, and who helped build up the athletics of the school. The versatile Erdman Olson who could drive a car, row a boat, give swimming lessons, and brighten up the life of the school with his harmless pranks, and who carried the high ideals of the school along with him. The fastidious dressed Olson whose parents were wealthy and who never lacked funds, and about whom it is said, 'no accounts about town are reported against him and his general deportment when off the college campus has no bad mark.'"

It was in that spirit that the article described his activities that weekend: "Erdman and some pals went to Winona early Saturday morning, September 25, and in the afternoon, they witnessed the football game between the Teachers College and Phalen Lutheran College of Minneapolis.

"Erdman and six of his college friends held a "party" after they attended the football game. The youths all returned to Galesville Saturday evening and showed evidences they had been drinking.

"The following day, September 26, Gale college observed its 25th anniversary under Lutheran control, and Erdman acted as usher in one of the auditoriums. He seemed calm, reserved, and unworried at that time."

Chris Olson was going to upset all of that. He knew that Erdman would not be attending any classes on Sunday, and he wanted some answers directly from his daughter's boyfriend. If he had to force a confrontation, then so be it, Chris told his Helgerson friends.

Oliver Helgerson parked the car on 12th Street of the small town of Galesville. Galesville was platted by Vermont-born Judge George Gale in 1854. He bought 2,000 acres, and chartered Gale University the same year. Judge Gale wanted a college for his son to attend, so the elegant Old Main building was opened for operation in 1862. He considered the spot in Trempealeau County to be so beautiful he called it the "Garden of Eden." The name stuck. Galesville served the surrounding farming and apple orchard community. Early on, Beaver Creek was dammed to create the 117-acre Lake Marinuka. Water from the lack powered a flour mill and sawmill.

Chris Olson approached Old Main and told the two Helgerson men to stay in the car.

Chris Olson recalled later the tone of the conversation. "I asked Erdman what he done with Clara. I asked him if he seen Clara that night. He said he hadn't. He said he never went down to get her. I told him I could prove it. He said, 'You can't prove nothing on me,' and then he started to go away. I said, 'You gave that girl instructions to burn your letters. ...' He kind of stopped and got kind of weak and asked me if I'd seen the letter. I said, 'Alice seen it.'

"I put my hand on his shoulder and I said, 'Erdman, I want to talk just a few minutes with you. You told her in the letter to meet you at the door at twelve o'clock, didn't you?' He said, 'I did.' I said, 'Now, perhaps you sent somebody else in your place to take her, because you called her out to the road.'

"He said he took her to Viroqua. I said I didn't believe it because I seen those auto tracks the next morning, and they came from the south.

"Then he said she went by bus from Viroqua to St. Paul. He said he gave her $50. He said that all is well with her, that she would be back again as soon as the baby was born."

Chris continued, "I told him I didn't have any strings on the girl. She was of age, and all I asked was that she write a few lines so we can see whether she is alive. He said he couldn't do that. I said, 'You got to bring her back so I can see if the girl is alive.'

"I said, 'Erdman, if there is anything between you and the girl that we don't know anything about, bring her back. I will help you all I can ...' I said, 'The two of you can go ahead and get married. I have plenty of room. I'll give a nice piece of ground and you can grow some tobacco and start you that way. Do the right thing and honorable thing,'" Chris told Erdman.

Chris was asked later exactly what he offered young Erdman. He said he offered the boy six cows, a team of horses, $500, and a home on his farm if he would marry his daughter. The youth, Chris Olson said, promised to marry the girl but wanted to wait a short time.

"He told me that if I would give him a little time, he could bring her back Thursday morning. I told him, 'Now you do down to the car and tell them, Oliver Helgerson and Andrew Helgerson, what you told me.'

"I told him, if the girl didn't show up in three days, by Thursday night. I would get the sheriff after him."

Newspaper reports later would state that Chris Olson and the two Helgerson men stayed at Gale College for three hours.

After the three farmers left, Erdman had a good laugh with some of his college friends about the old man's offer. He had often joked with his classmates about his relationship with Clara, whom he often called "a green, hick girl."

A hollow laugh it must have been, for Erdman Sanford Olson knew he was trapped. He had offered too many excuses and told too many lies. Yes, lies upon lies. He had lied to his parents, to Bernard Olson, who confronted him the morning of September 10, to his college friends, and now to Chris Olson, father of his slain lover. The biggest, most grievous lies, he had told his sweetheart.

Erdman's roommate later told reporters: "I heard him crying that night."

In the wee hours, Erdman sat at his dormitory desk and composed two letters. One to Chris Olson and one to his parents. He mailed them the next day. He boxed up some of his belongings, including his revolver, and sent them to his parents on that Monday morning.

Erdman approached Gale College president, K. Lokensgard, the same morning to announce that he was leaving school immediately. He claimed that he had to have a throat operation in La Crosse. With a small suitcase in hand, he left Gale College and was never seen again.

On Wednesday, September 29, 1926, Erdman Olson's parents received a final letter from their son.

> I suppose you heard a lot of things already. I know that I did. I had some visitors yesterday and they were real nice about some things. They seem to think that they have me where I can't wiggle my toes, which is where they are very much mistaken, very much so. He, the old man [Chris Olson], claims that he has absolute proof that I know where she is, and I haven't the least idea of her location, but I cooked up a story that she was in St. Paul, and that I would have to have some time to get her back here.
>
> I am leaving tonight for someplace where no one knows. I shall not even tell you folks, though, God knows, how I feel. I have thought of finishing everything but life is sweet and hard to part with, but I say this, that I shall rather take death than captivity.

I am taking the most necessary articles of clothing in a suitcase and I'm sending back the rest. This may seem like mockery but what else could I do with them? Give Orvid everything that he can use of my stuff. He is only one brother in a thousand, and it brings tears to think of what he has before him in the future. Poor little boy.

Some time I may write to you, but can't say that you will ever see me again, unless it may be in a coffin. Perhaps you may never want to see me again. I would not blame you if you don't. I have no money but got some checks that will do me for traveling expenses, until I get some work. I will never stay long in one place, for that would be dangerous.

Mother I suppose that your health will suffer tremendously from this, and it might wreck father, but don't let it do that

Live for Orvid; he will repay you many times for what you sacrifice for him. No child has ever had truer metal in it than he has. Forget me and live for Orvid. Send him to school and he will make you proud. These people cannot prove anything definite, although they will try. Do not let them try to pull anything over on you folks. Please try to bear this with bravery and forget me, as I am not worthy of your memory. Shut me out from your thoughts entirely, as though I never existed.

Good-by and God bless you all. You have not failed as parents, but I have failed as a son.

Erdman

PS. No one will ever know me by that name any more. Now it will be a different one. I told everyone that I'm going to the doctor for an operation. It is true that I will have to have another operation. Larson or Lokensgard will write you when I don't come back. Tell them what you please, it is immaterial to me.

Erdman penned another letter, this one to Clara's father:

I'll be at Gale no longer after tonight. I am going to make myself scarce enough so you cannot find me or Clara from now on. As far as I am concerned, just where she is, is my business. At the present and after the big bunch of lip I got from you, I am not caring a great deal, either.

There are things you'd better not try, and that is to drag my family into this matter, as they are entirely ignorant of those things, and if you don't want publicity, don't shout too loud, because it will not sound so awfully good to hear that your daughter run away in the night.

I believe she is all right in health and such, but where she is I can't say. I am leaving because I don't like the idea of the sheriff coming up here if I couldn't find her. I'll be back when she comes back.

After receiving the letter, Albert and Anna Olson visited the Chris Olson farm. Albert brought a rolled up *La Crosse Tribune* with a story about the missing girl, Clara Olson.

Albert chastised Chris for going to Galesville to harass his son. "They told me I made a bad mistake when I went up to Gale College," Chris said. "They said I'd threatened the boy and scared him out of school."

Chris was of no mind to listen to their accusations. His daughter was missing, and her boyfriend had written a very disturbing letter. On Tuesday September 28, he hired two detectives, Captain John T. Sullivan, retired Milwaukee chief of detectives and later to become chief of police in Kenosha. Captain Sullivan was known throughout the nation as an expert in crime fighting. He was tough, no nonsense, and meticulous.

The other person he hired was a Madison private detective, William Caswen, a retired police detective. For two months Caswen would check all medical facilities in Minneapolis, St. Paul, Milwaukee and other nearby cities. No record of Clara turned up anywhere.

Chris Olson and his son Bernard, however, would not merely wait for the professionals to turn up whatever evidence they could. On October 1, Bernard talked to fellow World War I veterans at the local VFW meeting house in Gays Mills. Chris Olson visited the grocery store in Mt. Sterling, asking anyone and everyone to be on the lookout for Clara Olson.

The father and son also called for search parties. Yet when a search of the Kickapoo Valley and the hills of the Driftless Region was suggested, the country folks of central Crawford County took it as a joke. You must be kidding! was the response. There were miles along the Bad Axe Creek, Buck Creek, Coulee Creek, Plum Creek, Bear Creek, Tainter Creek, Rush Creek, Nederloe Creek, Hornby Creek, Sugar Creek, Copper Creek, Hobbs Hollow, and a dozen other creeks and hollows.

Talk ran something like, "There's dozens, maybe hundreds, of places along the Kickapoo where a body could be weighted down and never found. Same as the Mississippi. Rope a rock around a person's middle, toss 'em in the river, the fish would have a feast." Then there are the impenetrable swamps, the caves, the precipitous bluffs.

There was snickering in the grocery stores, card parties, quilting bees, and church gatherings. Finding the body of Clara Olson, if it was buried in the area, would be harder than finding a needle in a haystack. Yet find her they would. Chris Olson had only just begun to look for his beloved daughter.

The home of Erdman Olson, near Rising Sun, was a half mile from where the body of Clara Olson was found Dec. 2, 1926.

CHAPTER 10
Missing Girl Is Big News

Day after day Chris Olson and his son Bernard could be seen tramping about the countryside, searching for any sign of Clara. The family was convinced that Clara Olson was dead, that Erdman Olson was the killer, and that he buried her somewhere in the area.

By this time the tobacco harvest was in, and the family had the time to look. Chris Olson had money, owning 317 acres of cultivated fields, woodland, and expensive tobacco land. According to an allotment system, a farmer was allowed a set number of acres for tobacco. Chris planted the maximum allowed. He would never divulge how many acres. It was a family enterprise, as his sons and daughters farmed with him.

Clara was missing, and the Olson family was determined to find her. Chris assumed she was dead, and he set out to prove it and to find her. Farm folks organized small posses. They would later be joined by others. He went to the county seat in Viroqua and hired a lawyer. He took the train to the state capital in Madison and hired two private detectives. He pestered the district attorney, J. S. Earll, at the Prairie du Chien county seat. Chris went to see him 15 times, rumor had it. District Attorney Earll was a hard-headed man, but Chris wore him down.

He talked to Justice of the Peace C. H. Speck as well. Speck was gruff, outspoken, and not easily swayed by any hypotheticals. Some declared that Speck was a mean S.O.B. "Proof. I want proof," he thundered during the cases brought before him.

On Thanksgiving Day, November 25, Chris Olson, with detectives Sullivan and Caswen, met with Sheriff Harry W. Sherwood and Judge C. H. Speck. Chris and the two detectives then conferred with newly elected Crawford County Sheriff Harry W. Underwood and D.A. J. S. Earll. The visitors laid out the evidence they had.

Doing business on Thanksgiving Day would be unbelievable by today's standards. Why would a sheriff and county justice meet with anyone on Thanksgiving Day? Sullivan and Caswen were not just anyone, especially Caswen. He had a reputation in crime fighting, known to anyone in Wisconsin politics, law enforcement, and the judicial process. He was a towering figure in criminal justice all over the Midwest. When Caswen asked for a meeting, Sheriff Sherwood and Justice Speck could not say no.

The evidence that Sullivan and Caswen and Chris Olson laid out when they visited on Thanksgiving Day centered on six main points:

1. The letter Erdman wrote to his parents. Caswen had the letter.
2. The letter Erdman wrote to Chris Olson.
3. Tire tracks found by Bernard on the morning of September 10.
4. Erdman changing his story.
5. No hospital reports of Clara's whereabouts.
6. Reports of Erdman's character from classmates.

Chris Olson and the two detectives meticulously went over the six points, one by one. Afterward, Chris filed a murder complaint against Erdman Olson. District Attorney Earll drew up a warrant, and Chris and his lawyer took it to the Justice of the Peace and had it properly sworn.

Justice Speck issued an arrest warrant for Erdman Olson based on "information and belief," even though a body had not been found. This step was unprecedented. A murder warrant had been issued with no body, no concrete evidence, no eyewitness, and no murder weapon. What they had was extremely strong: circumstantial evidence, motive, and a suspect that had fled.

The news exploded over the news wires on November 27, 1926. A sweetheart was missing, and her lover had skipped town. All the newspapers in the Midwest picked up the story. It made the wire services.

A murder warrant was a matter of public record, and no longer the ravings of a rumpled, disheveled Norwegian farmer in the hill country of southwestern Wisconsin.

The Tuesday, November 30, evening edition of the *Winona Republican Herald* displayed the bold headline: SEEK GALE COLLEGE STUDENT ON MURDER CHARGE. Radio stations considered it their lead story on every broadcast. Rewards were posted.

On Saturday, November 27, 1926, with the sheriff's consent, 600 men, most all farmers, formed a posse and began a search of the region. There was money on the line, a further reason to search for a body.

The warrant was a call to action. The *Prairie du Chien Courier* carried a long story. Legion to help organize a search for Clara's body, and Chris Olson offered a $200 reward.

The *Chicago Herald-Examiner*, a Hearst newspaper, latched onto this story with a vengeance. Not only did they have their ace crime reporter combing the hills of Crawford County for murder tidbits, they sent out Hamilton R. Bailey, who did the human interest, tear-jerking narratives. He interviewed the two Olson families, who were under extreme duress and emotion. The neighbors were mined for any nuggets of information. This was the era of tabloid newspapers, yellow journalism.

The news swept the countryside and indeed the entire nation. Several nearby farm boys were detained and questioned. Word came from Dwight, Illinois, of the arrest of a 22-year old farmhand. His detention prompted Sheriff Sherwood to board the train at Prairie du Chien and head for Chicago. The supposed killer had been spotted eating in a diner on Washington Street.

Going all out to sensationalize their coverage of the horrific crime, the *Herald-Examiner* hired a "character analyst and psychologist" whose studies the bumps and lines on Erdman Olson's photo. They conclude *"In Erdman Olson we have a combination of aggressive-receptive type, the male quality of aggressive at times offsetting the feminine which is receptive. Consequently, a youth of this type would frequently get himself into trouble."*

A blizzard was coming out of the north. The 200 American Legion and farmer searchers called off the search on Friday, November 26. They were peering into the thousands of nooks, caves, swamps, and frozen creeks that might hold the body.

The 200 promised, if the weather was favorable, to meet the next day at Stoney Point school to resume the search. Two areas of concern would be searched, covering yard by yard, the area near the boy's home at Rising Sun and then the neighborhood of the girl's farm residence near Seneca.

Believing that somewhere in the Crawford County hills, between the Kickapoo and the Mississippi, lay the body of Clara Olson, 22-year-old sweetheart of Erdman Olson, both of whom had been missing since their disappearance at midnight on September 9, a volunteer posse of from 50 to 100 men will start out in search over the territory tomorrow, said a newspaper report.

Sheriff Sherwood, at Prairie du Chien, announced today that the organized search would be a concerted effort on the part of friends of the Olson family to solve the mystery which had hung over the countryside since the night the girl left her home in company with Erdman Olson.

Two rewards, each for $200, were offered, one for the girl and one for the boy. Handbills announcing the reward for Erdman Olson were printed and distributed, one of them posted at the central police station in Prairie du Chien. Sheriff Sherwood was sending out 10,000 circulars to police forces around the country.

The latter offer carried this description of Erdman: "Age 18, weight, about 160 pounds, complexion light, height 5 feet 7.5 inches, blue eyes, dark brown hair, combed straight back, may be parted in the middle, may have a "V" scar on right side of face; blue eyes and has a habit of blinking, has habit of standing first on one foot and then the other, recently had a nasal operation and both tonsils removed and two teeth extracted. Nationality: native-born Norwegian descent. Was a student at Gale College, from which he disappeared September 27."

Rumors emanating from Prairie du Chien that Erdman Olson, charged in a warrant with slaying the girl, was seen in the vicinity of the border line of Iowa were denied in a telephone conversation with Sheriff Sherwood later in the day. He stated that the search for Clara Olson's body, since she was believed to have slain, would begin early the next morning by volunteer searchers and continue throughout the day.

***

Meanwhile, the private detectives employed by Olson were scouting other possibilities of the missing woman's whereabouts on the chance that her death was not established without finding the body. Two theories concerning possible solution of the mystery were advanced by searchers. One supported the theory of Chris Olson that the girl had been slain. The other was that she was in a hospital in the Twin Cities, where Erdman told Chris Olson he had sent her.

Albert Olson came to the defense of his son after the warrant charging murder had been issued. He revealed that he had closely inspected the lad's automobile and had found no marks or stains that indicated that a murder had taken place in it. "This whole thing" he said, "grows out of an effort to make my boy marry Clara Olson. I don't care how this turns out, they'll find my boy committed no crime."

Lack of concrete information would lead to a number of wild-goose chases. One group of searchers was accompanied by James S. Holmes. He remembers seeing a coat, a woman's stocking, and a woman's shoes on an island in the Mississippi

River in September, just after Clara Olson vanished. The river was swollen, the waters had inundated the isle, and the surface had frozen, leaving the island covered with several inches of ice. Holmes was certain the coat was plush. But it was revealed that Clara Olson had no such coat, but instead wore a tan spring coat that night.

Following her disappearance, the father interpreted the note she left behind to mean she would be back soon, and that she would have a "glad surprise" when she returned and would have married Erdman Olson. Clara's brother, Arthur Olson, 28, went to Milwaukee, today seeking friends who Clara visited there a few years earlier. It was his forlorn hope that his sister, if alive, might have communicated with them. However, he, like his father, truly believed she was dead.

The following story in the November 30 issue of the *Prairie du Chien Courier Press* summarized the Olson murder story to date. Among other information the article reported that after Erdman disappeared, "Later it is said checks were cashed in Minneapolis on one of the banks which gave searchers the first clue of his whereabouts."

Another report said that Erdman Olson had been seen in Iowa. Another story had authorities turning their attention to quack hospitals and quack doctors They were probing every medical institution believing it possible that the girl may have fallen a victim to illegal practices.

Authorities also were seeking an accomplice who had aided and abetted the Gale College youth in spiriting away his sweetheart. Investigators were sent to Viroqua to determine if the girl was actually brought there, as Erdman Olson was reported to say she was; also, at La Crosse, Winona police were notified and given a description of the girl and the youth.

Authorities soon learned that Clara had received letters from Erdman almost every day, and that after receiving one on September 9, her sister Alice saw her burning all the letters. Her sister also said she saw Clara fix a light near the window and experimented pulling the shade up and down, indicating she was carrying out a signal code.

From campus comrades, detectives learned that Erdman always carried a pistol, even to college affairs and dances. He never explained the reason for this, they said. The youth was not popular, even in his hometown of Rising Sun. He was "peculiar" and "cold," stubborn and uncommunicative, the young folk of the locality said. Erdman and Clara kept company for a year and a half, yet never appeared together at dances or parties. "Olson was a quiet boy and was behind in his studies," President K. Lokensgard of Gale College said. "Because he was behind in his work, he was not in any special class."

In the meantime, the post-harvest cycle wound on. During the week starting on November 25, the weather was mild with high humidity. The Norwegian tobacco farmers knew that it was "casing weather." Time to remove the tobacco laths from the shed, strip the leaves from their stems, and lay them in wooden boxes or cases. The temperature on November 30 reached 44 degrees as tobacco was sent to the warehouses in Viroqua.

With a lack of results, farmers, shop owners, and sheriff's deputies abandoned the search for Clara in the Kickapoo Valley. The mid-40s temperatures sent streams of water flowing down from the snow-capped hills, turning them into wet and slippery area of mud. Truth be told, it was difficult to get people enthused about a search for a girl that most believed was not dead. They were puzzled by the strange actions of Erdman Olson but believed both he and Clara would return in a few days or weeks. They believed that Clara Olson was merely heartbroken and disgraced, feeling keenly the shame of her love affair with Erdman Olson, and that she would return when the storm was over.

On Tuesday, November 30, a warrant was issued for Erdman Olson. Chris Olson offered a $200 reward for finding his daughter. Circumstances were about to change. While on this blustery last day in November, the fate of Clara Olson remained in limbo, a new push would be made that yielded a more definite conclusion.

Albert Olson family and hired man: L-R, Edwin Knutson, hired man, Albert Olson, Anna Olson, and Erdman's 11 year-old brother, Arvid, in the foreground.

CHAPTER 11

Clara Olson Found Dead

The *Chicago Herald-Examiner* carried the story about the latest search for Clara Olson with a big headline: OLSON POSSE BATTLES BLIZZARD.

Bernard and Adolph had taken the matter to the American Legion in Gays Mills. Subsequently, the post called for volunteers, and hundreds of men stepped forward. Snow was falling as some 200 searched on Wednesday, December 1. With a warning of a blizzard that was howling out of the north, the search was quickly abandoned.

The big search began in the early hours of Thursday, December 2, after the cows were milked and the livestock watered and fed. Most all the crops were in, with only scattered shocks of standing corn here and there.

By the following day, the Kickapoo Valley might be blanketed with heavy snow, lending further difficulties to the search for the girl's body. After tracking through the thousands of nooks, caves, swamps, and frozen creeks that might hold the body, the searchers had found no trace of the girl.

The predicted snowstorm held off, however, and the search began again on December 2. The American Legion mobilized to comb the Kickapoo Valley. The posse was believed to have swelled to over 1,000 men and boys from the farms and villages of Crawford County. In charge was W. W. Coon, a former commander of the post. The posse divided itself into three groups, one setting out in the direction of the Chris Olson home, another on a southerly angle, and a third took off in a short route to the north of Mt. Sterling, focusing on the vicinity of the extensive farm lands owned by Albert Olson. Bernard remembered in particular where Erdman Olson's car had been pulled to the side of the road, so 30 men penetrated the depths of the nearby woods.

The marshes of the Winnishiek were thoroughly combed. The posse searched every foot of the territory, including the deep woods, the cliffs, and the caves. The search parties were led by men experienced in covering the rough country of western Wisconsin. They declared, before they started out, that if the young girl was murdered and her body hidden among the hills, it would be found by nightfall.

A posse of 600 men in small groups walked north from Seneca along Highway 27 toward Rising Sun, a distance of six miles. Men and boys searched through caves on the farms. Men dug on several farms, according to one account. Any freshly turned earth was suspect as well as rumors that people were seen digging, such as for the burial of pets.

By appointment, a party of searchers, numbering nearly two hundred, met at Stoney Point School, a crossroads on the main highway two miles south of Mt. Sterling, Stoney Point, which drew its name from a peculiar rock formation, was in full view of Clara Olson's home. Clara, in fact, was educated at the school.

By this point the search for the body had become a big story. Newspapers from all over the Midwest sent reporters to Prairie du Chien, the Crawford County seat of government. Most came by railroad and filled up the few hotels. From Prairie du Chien, they fanned out across the Seneca, Mt. Sterling, and Rising Sun countryside. A few, with their rented cars parked along Highway 27, joined in the search.

The *Chicago Herald-Examiner*, a Hearst newspaper, sent several reporters to southwest Wisconsin. The front page of the December 1, 1926, *Herald-Examiner* had a story penned by newspaperman Harold L. Polland. "Meanwhile search for the girl was carried on by farmers and townspeople who are spread in a great posse all through the woods and purple hills of the picturesque Kickapoo Valley." One group dug and searched the Tulley Farm, near Rising Sun, where the young Gale College student lived, and "whose lonely precincts have provided ghostly tales and eerie noises for the country folk."

Who discovered the grave? It depends on whose account you read. The chance for some measure of fame would induce a number of men to step forward and make a claim. The following account was the most readily accepted.

Four days earlier, on the afternoon of November 28, 1926, Clarence Allen, one of Clara's cousins, had been walking next to his friend, Hillman Lee. They reached the crest of a hill called Battle Ridge. Chief Blackhawk, a leader of several Native American tribes, principally Sauk, had taken a stand there back in 1832. They took the high ground and fended off pursuing U.S. troops, fighting a rear guard action to allow the tribes' women, children, and old men to move toward the Mississippi River. People still found bones scattered among the oaks. The ground was stony, thick with the roots of red and black oak trees. Clarence stumbled on a root, looked down, and kept walking. They said later that they had been hunting for Clara's body and had walked right over her grave.

Four days later, around 10:30 in the morning, the temperature was climbing from a low of 24 degrees to a high of near 30. The sky was overcast with low stratus clouds. Charles Bown, woodsman and farmer, was leading a detail of two other men, Michael O'Leary of Gays Mills and Edward Chitwood of Soldiers Grove. Bown accidentally came upon the spot and, with his fellow searchers, he paused momentarily to view the surrounding landscape from that commanding point. Anyone less trained in woodcraft might have not seen or noticed the grave at all. He later said that the ground looked unnatural to him.

Bown saw a bit of turf turned and looked down to see where Clarence Allen had stumbled several days earlier. The yellow mud was frozen, but it was a sign that someone had turned the earth. The acid reaction between ferric hydroxide and the humus gave rise to the yellow color.

Bown started to poke the spot with a stick. After a few dexterous turns, Bown was awed by the exposure of a woman's heel encased in a new rubber boot.

He called to O'Leary and Chitwood, who were searching nearby. "The search is over! She's down here!" Bown shouted.

The two men ran over to the spot where he pointed. The heels of new rubber boots protruded out of the yellow subsoil. It was known Clara had worn new boots when she slipped out of her father's house on the night she went to meet her sweetheart, Erdman, because searchers had been given a description of the clothing Clara wore the night she disappeared.

Soon several hundred searchers were acquainted with the fact that Clara Olson's body had been found. The party moved more dirt, uncovering more of the body. The clothes they saw matched the description of the clothing Clara wore on that fateful night nearly 12 weeks ago. It was Clara, all right.

"Let's not disturb this grave any further," someone in the crowd called out. They were sufficiently aware that trained people were needed. Do not destroy any possible evidence.

One of the party ran 40 yards to the highway and flagged down a passing motorist. News traveled up and down the ridges and valleys, and within an hour everyone knew. Clara Olson had been found, and she was dead. No information about the way in which Clara met her death was available. One of the search party was sent to Mt. Sterling to telephone authorities in Prairie du Chien.

As the news spread, more searchers converged on the spot. Men stopped their cars along Highway 27. No one touched the grave, though. The grave was shallow and long. "It took time to dig a grave like that, cutting through roots with an axe. Must have been prepared in advance," mused one of the farmers.

Soon other men came along, and in a short while a crowd of silent and sober-faced farmers had gathered around the grave. Automobiles on the state highway, forty rods, some 600 feet, from the grave were stopping and told to carry the news through the county.

The crowd gathered around the slightly sunken spot on the top of drab Battle Ridge, land owned, by the way, by Erdman's uncle, Nels Severson. The farmers told one another in awed whispers that old Chris Olson's dream visions had come true.

No rosed-hued dream that, but one of tragedy and death. "I've seen Clara," old Chris had declared. "I've seen her in a dream. I know she's dead. I saw her buried on her face in a grave on a hill near Rising Sun."

Battle Ridge was only one mile south of Rising Sun.

The Coroner Takes Charge

Coroner Frank Holly of Prairie du Chien was notified by telephone that the body had been found. With coroner-elect Ernest Otteson, he left for Mount Sterling.

No examination was attempted before their arrival. The body was merely covered up from the eyes of the curious.

The two authorities proceeded to the "Woods of Death." When Holley arrived, he made a minute examination of the scene and took statements of the searching party. By that time, 300 men and boys had gathered around the grave. They had laid dead branches framing it, out of respect. Night was coming on, and a light snow was falling.

Coroner Holly brought a spade with him. A sturdy young farmer with an overseas cap on his head and a soldier's overcoat seized the spade and begin digging a trench around the spot, now marked off with four dried branches. Two other young men retrieved shovels from their cars and joined in.

They didn't have to dig very deep. The body was only a foot or so down. It lay tumbled facedown. The men with the shovels dug deeper. Before long it became evident that they would have no trouble about the identification: a part of the tan lightweight coat that Clara wore away from home and some of the red sweater she wore under the coat came away from the dirt and clay. The light stockings were seen.

The grave was opened in the heavy clay soil through which a thick network of roots of red and white oak trees ran. A mass of roots of all sizes, some of which had to be cut through with an ax, protruded from the jagged and roughly hewn edges of the gouged-out tomb. When the trench was nearly three feet deep on all sides, the ground beneath the body was excavated away, and willing hands supported the corpse.

At the coroner's signal, the men lifted Clara and laid her in a long shallow wicker basket. They were careful not to brush the mud from her clothes. Clara's left hand was clenched against her chest. Her right hand dangled down. A farmer picked it up and gingerly laid it across Clara's stomach. Only a few low whispers broke the silence among the throng of searchers, in this cathedral of lofty oaks, some pressing in to get a glance of the grave site.

A little purse was found hanging from the belt of her dress. The men were careful not to leave anything behind. Kerosene lanterns illuminated the bottom of the grave. The body was fully clothed. It was dressed in a black silk dress, a new one Miss Olson purchased the day she went away. Her tan-gray spring coat was thrown over the body. Pieces of the pearl necklace on which her father had depended much for identification, had the elements made it otherwise impossible, were found beside her.

In the gloom of the early winter afternoon, men could see the flicker of lights from the Albert Olson farmstead. But Erdman was not there. He had disappeared from the face of the earth 66 days ago.

The body was removed from the grave and taken to the Paul Dommersnaes funeral parlor in Mt. Sterling, a trek of six miles. Most of the crowd followed. Soon they were gathered in a growing knot around the undertaker's door. The undertaker had orders from the coroner to let no one in.

Finding the body of the missing girl was dramatic. The keen eye of one man had noticed a shallow low ditch, covered with snow, on a forty-acre tract wooded with a second growth of white oak. The crude sepulcher was dug on Battle Ridge Hill, ten rods east of the main state highway W-27, just a quarter of mile from the home of Albert Olson.

A logging road led from the main highway, the Black River Road (Highway 27), into the obscure place. The grave, thirty-five feet off that old logging road, was dug a sufficient distance from the logging road that is would not be spotted by a walker, hunter, or rider in any vehicle.

The location weakened the defense offered later by Erdman's parents that he would not have had time to kill the girl, dispose of her body, and reach his home at 1:15 or 1:30 A.M. as he did. The timing worked out logically. He left the Chris Olson home at midnight. The distance from the Clara's farmhouse to the grave site was 10 miles. The student's home, one quarter mile, as the crow flies, was but one-half mile by road. The slaying and burying of the girl and the drive to the grave and home easily could have been done in an hour and a half, authorities would say.

Clara Olson had been found and now would receive a proper Christian funeral service and burial in the Utica Norwegian Lutheran Church graveyard. Next to her body was an instrument, yet undiscovered by the authorities, that would name her killer.

(Top) *The body of Clara Olson was placed in wicker basket and taken to the Dommersnaes Funeral Parlor in Mt. Sterling to await identification by Chris Olson.*
(Bottom) *The grainy photo, taken before the body of Clara Olson was lifted from the grave, was sent to newspapers across America. The photo shows a member of the sheriff's posse which totaled over 1000 men and boys.*

CHAPTER 12

How Did She Die?

News reached the Chris and Dina Olson household shortly before noon. A body had been discovered buried off the highway south of Rising Sun. It had been taken to the Paul T. Dommersnaes, a licensed embalmer at the Mt. Sterling Furniture and Undertaking Establishment. Ironically, a few doors away was the Jas. Brockway & Co., which had sold the Ford Roadster driven by Erdman Olson.

Would Chris come to identify the body? He tried to cheer up his wife, patted her on the shoulder, "Cheer up, Ma," he said. "You'll see. It ain't her."

Mrs. Olson rocked furiously back and forth before the window where her chair had been most of the time since their daughter had vanished three months ago. Yet even though the three other daughters screamed hysterically, the aged mother could not cry.

Stern old Chris Olson, so certain that his daughter Clara would be found, stoically bid goodbye to his wife and walked out the door. The mask soon dropped. When he was out of sight, he broke down and cried like a child. He staggered forward and would have collapsed had not neighbors caught him and carried him to an automobile.

"My little girl! My little Clara!," cried the father. He sobbed quietly during the 10-minute drive north to Mt. Sterling.

He was taken to the Dommersnaes mortuary, where the body of Clara, stained with frozen earth, lay. Chris, leaning on the arm of his son Bernard came, and the crowd milling around parted. Chris braced himself and walked inside.

Recognition was instantaneous. He saw Clara's new shoes, worn only twice, once to church and the night she went to her death. He gazed at the blackened, muddy form, the new rubbers on the shoes, the tan coat, the red sweater. He recognized remnants of her summer coat.

"It's her!," he gasped. "It's Clara. Oh, I knew she was dead. I knew it!" he moaned.

Then the 60-year-old man fainted, falling into his son's arms. Chris was carried outside, where he soon revived. In a daze he walked across the street, leaned against a tree, and wept.

The grief-stricken father, sobbing, too weak to stand alone, was approached by the District Attorney–elect Arthur Curran. "This will be my case," said Curran, "and I promise you faithfully that I will be bring Clara's murderer to justice." The old man nodded tearfully.

People in the crowd were struck by the story of his dream told two weeks earlier to friends. One of them, Mae King of Mt. Sterling, related, "I saw her in my dreams. She was lying facedown in her grave. That is exactly how and where she was found."

Seeing the father weeping, the crowd muttered threats against the youth accused of Clara's murder. "When we find that son-of-a-bitch, there will be a rope waiting for 'im." "That cowardly bastard ..." "He's a goddamn evil ..."

Back home, lying on a couch and still weeping, the aged man issued a remarkable statement. "I forgive young Olson," he said. "I forgive his father. I forgive them all. My family is better off now than his is, even if my little Clara is gone."

Still the white-haired mother continued rocking. She had not cried. Her children and friends were fearful for the aged couple. Would the murder of their daughter lead to more deaths?

Albert Olson Responds

Reporters visited the Albert Olson farm the day after the discovery of Clara's body. In the face of the recent developments, Erdman's father calmly maintained his son's innocence, as he had done all along. He remained on his farm during the excitement attending the discovery of the body.

All that commotion from noon on was just a quarter mile west of his farm buildings. He and wife Anna could see and hear the buzz of activity with all the cars coming and going.

Albert Olson was asked about Erdman and Clara. "Of course," he said, "everybody would expect me to say what I'm saying. But I'm not saying it because it is the natural or expected thing, but because I'm convinced of it."

"Puts you in a kind of a hole, Mr. Olson, doesn't it?" someone asked.

"Yes," he said. "It does. But what can I do? You can't tell me that boy could kill that girl, come home right from up there on the hill, and tune into the radio and look at the mail order catalogs."

Did he have any possible explanation? No-o-o-o, he couldn't think of any except, "Perhaps some one of Erdman's enemies killed the girl and buried her body there on his uncle's place so near his own house. Someone who knew circumstances, how they were after Erdman to marry that girl, and knew he could easily throw suspicion of him. Anyway, Erdman didn't do it. It'll all come out in time, you'll see."

Meantime, people in the village of Mt. Sterling were discussing the open, shallow grave up on Battle Ridge. They were saying that timber up on the ridge was always a bad spot.

"Why," said one old man, "forty years ago, a man took two horses up there and tied 'em to a tree and they starved there. Right there, practically on the ground where the body was found. He tied 'em and they ate all the grass as far as they could reach by lying down and stretching out their necks and even their lips until they couldn't reach it anymore and so they died."

Another old-timer recalled, "About 10 years ago, there was another murder up there on that knoll. About the same spot they found that girl. Wild hogs ate the body." Yet another claimed, "I knew that Battle Ridge was haunted."

Up and down the hills and valleys of Crawford County there was no lack of speculation on the cause of death. Rumors were rampant. No marks of external violence had been seen through that coating of frozen earth, and the theory of poison as the instrument of murder briefly occupied the authorities' attention.

They ordered searches of the home of Albert Olson, where deadly poisonous nicotine was used as a plant spray. Perhaps one-half to one ounce of that powerful drug, mixed, in a flask of whisky or gin, would create a lethal dose, paralyzing the heart. A toast to the wedding she believed was to climax her adventurous flight at midnight with young Olson might have accomplished her death.

If Clara had drank that, physical paralysis and death would have followed so swiftly that she could have been carried, as she must have been, 30 feet from an old logging road in the woods to the barren spot where she was thrown, facedown, into the grave. The rumors were endless.

One question voiced from many quarters was, "Why did so much time pass between the girl's disappearance until the issuing of the warrant for the arrest of Erdman Olson?" That period had lasted from September 10 to November 26, a period of 77 days.

Part of the reason stemmed from the highly unusual occurrence of a murder in these parts. Crawford County had a population of only 23,472. All but the 3,500 residents of Prairie du Chien lived on farms or in the ten villages numbering less than 500 apiece. It was a community of industrious, peace-loving folk, and any type of crime was rare.

The main reason, though, was the uncertainty regarding Clara's disappearance. Six weeks prior to the issuance of the warrant, District Attorney Earll and Sheriff Sherwood had visited both Olson families for what meager information they could glean. From these interviews they became convinced that

Clara and Erdman were unharmed and would return with their baby in due time. Apparently, Albert and Anna Olson did not turn over to authorities the final letter that Erdman wrote to them. No sign of a crime was evident, and only after the efforts of private detective William Caswen, who brought to light many new angles and evidence in the case—such as the letters written to both parents, the tire tracks found by Bernard, Erdman changing his story, as well as the lack of reports from any hospital of Clara's whereabouts—was it possible for the county officials to issue a warrant for the arrest of Erdman on a charge of murder.

Regardless of official caution, the discovery of her body opened the floodgates of media coverage. All of the reporters who had come to southwestern Wisconsin had been rewarded. The news was broadcast far and wide.

One newspaper reported, "The issuance of the warrant for the arrest of Erdman Olson by Justice Speck on November 26 on the petition of the bereaved father and evidence of William Caswen, a former operative with a detective agency, coupled with the nationwide publicity of metropolitan newspapers, resulted in the gruesome find of the dead body of Clara Olson December 2, 1926."

The *Chicago Herald Examiner* of Friday, December 3, used the largest possible type: CLARA OLSON SLAIN IN WOODS; VIEW BOY'S NOTE AS CONFESSION.

Subheadline: "Grave Near Home Yields Girl's Body; Auto Gives Clue"

Below that ran: "Mystery Clouds Cause of Death; Poison Theory is Held; Autopsy Today"

The dateline listed: Harold L. Polland, Prairie Du Chien, Wis Dec 2.

The frozen earth of Kickapoo Valley, which held the body of Clara Dorothy Olson, 22-year old country girl, for nearly three months while the countryside sought her, still clung tonight the secret of manner of her death.

Whether it covers the marks of a clubbed weapon, the wound of a gunshot, the searing brand of acid or trace of the poison must wait until tomorrow afternoon the reveal by an official autopsy.

The full text of the lad's farewell message to his parents, written on the night before he fled on September 27, was made public tonight. Authorities, who issued the murder warrant chiefly on its sinister wording, view it as a virtual confession.

It warns the parents that many things "not nice" will be told of him, that he was going away forever, and that he would choose death "rather than captivity".

Search for the Gale College student, more or less apathetic, since there was no body to prove murder, took on the aspect of vigorous action tonight. Sheriff Harry Sherwood prepared to seize the youth's automobile, following the discovery by a newspaper reporter that there were stains on the inside of the car's right-hand door.

The same reporter late today interviewed the father, who steadfastly contends his son is innocent, and was led to the garage and walked about the car. As he opened the right-hand door, however, the father closed the garage door, shutting out the light.

But in the flare of lighted matches, the stains were clearly visible. Officials were planning to question closely the father of the boy.

Another story in the *Chicago Herald Examiner* that day had the headline: FATHER STILL SURE ERDMAN IS INNOCENT.

The subheading declared: "Third Party Killed Clara, Says Planter: Blames Threats For Disappearance of His Son."

With a dateline of Rising Sun, Wi, dated Dec 2, the story reported:

Finding the body of Clara Dorothy Olson today failed to shake the faith of Albert Olson, wealthy tobacco planter, in the innocence of his son, the fugitive Erdman Sanford Olson, sweetheart of Clara.

"I'll believe he is innocent until he convinces me by his own words that he is not," said Mr. Olson.

"A third person killed Miss Olson. My son did not do it, and I can prove it. I can prove that his clothes bore no stains or dirt or anything else on the night she disappeared. Neither did his shoes. There is nothing to link him to this crime He had no way of getting implements to dig a grave. He is innocent. And I will stick by him to the last."

Erdman had other love affairs, his father said, and if he was the sweetheart of Clara, it was not his first romance.

"I don't know where Erdman is," continued his farther. "I haven't heard from him since he left. He left because he was threatened by Chris Olson. He threatened my boy because he wouldn't marry Clara. He was heard to threaten him."

Erdman feared Olson's threats, particularly about sending the sheriff and he did what any young boy probably would do, he ran away.

"I'm glad for his sake, though, that he is not here now. Feeling is running high against him, I know."

Mr. Olson had heard mutterings of the crowd, for as the body was borne from its grave, shouts of "Lynch him," "String him up," came from the searchers.

The next edition of the *Prairie du Chien Courier Press* printed a curious editorial:

In the eyes of society 50 years behind the mode of actual practice, Clara Olson, a sweet country girl, because of her habitual close-to-home rural surroundings, lacked the knowledge of birth control so generally practiced by her city cousins, and the fear of shame caused by an equally rural youth to foully commit murder. Until birth control laws are framed to conform modern practices, society will criminally brand every girl who makes a single mistake and more ruthless murders will result.

The manner of Clara Olson's death was not yet known. Now she was free of that sepulcher, awaiting an autopsy and release of information that will indict her killer. Clara Olson would receive a Christian burial after being interred on Battle Ridge for 82 days.

Newspapers employed artists to sketch events that could not be photographed. Such an artist's rendition shows Erdman Olson being driven back to Gale College by hired hand Edwin Knutson.

CHAPTER 13

The Autopsy

The body of Clara Olson was moved from Mt. Sterling to Prairie du Chien late on Thursday, December 2, 1926. Scores of farmers and searchers had followed the vehicle carrying her body, carefully encased in the wicker basket, from its crude grave on Battle Ridge to the undertaker's parlor. Now in darkness, the body was brought to the county capital. It was hoped that Dr. Charles H. Bunting, famed state pathologist at the University of Wisconsin in Madison, would conduct the autopsy the next day.

Clara Olson remained in the wicker basket at a local funeral home. Next to her bosom she carried a message that would indict her killer. The crowds were anxious to hear the cause of death. When informed that no news of how the young woman met her death could be learned immediately, they filed back to their homes in darkness of the night.

All day Friday, the body awaited the autopsy. A coroner's inquest to determine how Clara died was to follow. A superficial examination revealed no bullet wound or bruise from a blow, and officials began discussing poison as a possibility.

District Attorney J. S. Earll came back that day from Chicago to take charge of the investigation. He had been attending the International Livestock Exposition when advised that the body of the girl had been found. He cut short his visit.

The authorities in Prairie du Chien wanted to obtain the services of Dr. Bunting, of Madison, but Earll had made up his mind that if the doctor could not perform the duties, he was prepared to hire a group of local doctors to do the autopsy. Still, this was turning into a high-profile case, covered by every newspaper and radio outlet in the United States and many overseas. He did not want to make a mistake or later be deemed negligent.

As the *Chicago Tribune* put it, "Authorities of this quiet valley, called on for the first time to officiate in a murder where mystery has been a large element, have been fearful that clumsy hands might mar what evidence there is to point to Clara's slayer. And so the body has lain, face down, in the long basket, as it was found, untouched and clothed as it was when neighbors dug it up."

Finally, word reached Earll from Madison that Dr. Bunting could not arrive on Friday but would be coming by train on Saturday morning to make an examination. His findings would be put before the coroner's jury later in the day. He was expected to answer the question, still undecided: How did Clara Olson die? No thorough examination of the body was made, pending Dr. Bunting's arrival. The body was held in the Otteson Funeral establishment. Even the owner of the establishment was excluded by two deputies, posted by the district attorney.

The post-mortem examination was scheduled for ten o'clock. Coroner Frank Holley was to be in charge of an inquest at two o'clock in the afternoon. Crowds—mostly friends, newspaper reporters, and the curious—gathered around the building on Saturday morning.

Dr. Bunting found Clara Olson in the same condition that a posse discovered her in the grave on historic Battle Ridge. The protective coating of black soil that had received her on the tragic night she fled from her parents' home off Stoney Point still clung to her body and had all evidence of the manner of her death.

As the autopsy began, newspapermen and others interested were permitted to enter and remain in the front room of the building. When eager ears of press men, however, were able to catch most of the dictation of Dr. Bunting to a stenographer as he examined the body, District Attorney Earll ordered the room cleared.

Turned out into the cold street with a blizzard beating down, a number of newspapermen took up a new position across the street, in the Imperial Ice Cream parlor, through the windows of which they watched for the appearance of the district attorney and the jury, which would indicate that the examination was complete.

Occasionally one of the locals, unaware that the admittance to the building had been prohibited, sifted through the cordon of newspapermen grouped about the entrance awaiting word from within, only to be met by a barred door.

"They aren't letting anyone in, I guess," was their common expression as they were turned away.

In addition to Dr. Bunting, Crawford County Sheriff Sherwood and Mr. Earll asked three local physicians, Dr. J. J. Kane, Dr. F. J. Antoine, and Dr. C. A. Armstrong, to assist. As the doctors lifted Clara's body onto the autopsy table, the pearls from her necklace scattered across the surface. A tiny bottle of perfume fell out of her purse. Dr. Bunting retrieved the pearls and placed them in a little pan. He tightened the cap of the perfume bottle and set it in another pan.

He noted Clara's clothing: tan coat, greenish-black silk dress, red wool sweater, new shoes, new stockings, new undergarment. All were noted and taken by dictation by a court reporter. All items were tagged and set aside.

When Dr. Bunting removed the sticky clay dirt from her body, a thick wad of paper tumbled out of her bodice. It was a damp, gory mass. Dr. Bunting used tweezers to lift the wad of paper up to the light. Two letters were found stuffed in her bosom. The doctors could see that the words written on it were in purple ink. Dr. Bunting placed the wad on an enamel tray.

Dr. Bunting began his examination of the cadaver. "Terrific crushing blows to the head" were the direct cause of death. As Dr. Bunting rotated the head, a two-and-a-half-inch piece of bone fell from the left side of the skull onto the table. There were multiple severe fractures of the left temple and a single fracture on the right. It appeared that Clara had been struck from behind. A single blow from a heavy ax, club, hammer, or pipe might have caused the injuries, but the doctor thought it was more likely that "a series of blows had been struck." There was no evidence of rape. No evidence of abortion. Clara had been six months pregnant when she died. The child she carried was a girl.

Dr. Bunting asked the newly elected district attorney, Arthur Curran, to come in. The doctor wanted him to be present when he unfolded the paper that had fallen from Clara's bodice. They carefully separated and cleaned the paper, revealing the letter Erdman had sent her on September 7, instructing her what to do two days later. She hadn't destroyed this one, instead taking it along perhaps to retain as a keepsake for the happy years she expected would follow.

The inquest into the cause of death of Clara Olson was called at 4:30 in the courtroom of Magistrate C. H. Beck, deputized by Coroner Frank Holly, to hear the evidence after the autopsy. The coroner, who made his living as a barber, was too busy with his Saturday trade to attend. The testimony was given instead by the four attending the autopsy, led by Dr. Bunting. Once his work was completed, the doctor was anxious to catch the last train to Madison Saturday evening.

The physicians had worked over the body and completed their work in three hours. Dr. Bunting, after being sworn, was the first to take the stand. C. H. Speck, Justice of the Peace, who issued the murder warrant, presided over the jury. J. S. Earll, District Attorney, conducted the examination. On the inquest jury were six prominent locals, all men: Henry Otto, insurance agent; Roy Scheckler, undertaker; Tom Gander, register of deeds; Edward McCloskey, merchant; John Peacock, pearl dealer; and Leo LaPointe, butcher.

Dr. Bunting testified that he had been a pathologist for 18 years and had conducted many postmortem examinations. He said that the body of the deceased was fully clothed. He went on to describe in great detail every piece of clothing: brown knit jacket, a red knit sweater, black silk dress with short sleeves, black stockings, shoes and rubbers, and undergarments. The silk dress that Clara had purchased was believed to be her intended wedding dress. There was a ring on one finger. The pocket of the dress, according to Dr. Armstrong, contained an empty purse and a small bottle of perfume. The girl's right hand was folded across her breast, testimony showed.

A string of imitation pearls had been removed around her neck, but the string was broken. Dr. Bunting did not emphasize this, although the jury showed great interest, leaning forward to catch the best glimpse possible. Showing the thin rope with the break in the beads, Dr. Bunting indicated to the jury that a struggle might have taken place. He also disclosed that Clara Olson was wearing a maternity corset. He said that Clara would be a mother, had she lived. The baby was a girl and would have been born shortly after Christmas.

Dr. Bunting described the lungs and the liver, telling the jury that there was no sign of poisoning. One or more terrific blows killed the girl, and the blows were probably struck from behind. He reported a series of fractures over the left ear, partially toward the back on her skull, and a slight fracture on the right side.

"Probably there was more than one blow," Dr. Bunting said," for only a blow of terrific force would cause so many fractures." Death was instantaneous, he said. The testimony of the doctor was the first revelation of how the girl died,

Dr. Bunting testified that a great portion of the left side of the skull had been crushed in by a terrific blow or blows in the region of the left ear. He said he found no pathological conditions within the body which would have resulted in death.

In response to a question asked by District Attorney Earll, regarding the possibility that the girl might have been killed in a fall, Dr. Bunting indicated that would necessarily have to be from a great height. "If she had fallen from a sixth- or seventh-story building directly on that side of her head, it might have caused a fracture of that nature," he said, "but not a fall from a hill or a cliff."

That the skull had not been pierced by a sharp object, but rather with a blunt instrument, was the theory advanced by the experts. Dr. Bunting also said it was likely that the girl was struck with "one terrific blow."

Assisting Dr. Bunting in the autopsy conducted behind closed doors were Drs. C. A. Armstrong and J. J. Kane, both of Prairie du Chien—the latter being a physician in the sanitarium—and Dr. F. J. Antoine. Dr. Kane gave a technical description of the body for the record.

The four doctors who conducted the autopsy did mention the wad of blood-soaked letters found on Clara's body. They did not reveal the contents of those letters. That was left to District Attorney Earll.

Erdman's last letter to Clara, the one that told her, twice, to burn all his letters, would, as it turned out, seal his fate. It zipped up the case as to the identity of the killer. Though they were physicians holding the autopsy, they had uncovered the most important evidence since the body of Clara Olson was found murdered.

The importance of the pencil-scribbled note from Erdman was stressed by District Attorney Earll, who refused to make its text public until after the inquest the next day. Earll told reporters that letters were found, but would not tell of the contents. "The letter puts the entire case in a different light," he said. "I cannot tell you what it contains until I have brought in several witnesses whose presence is made necessary by its contents. No one will see it until these witnesses have been found.

"I can only tell you that it is so sensational that it suggests an entirely new theory of this murder, and that I believe it to be of the utmost significance."

"It was the last letter from Erdman Olson to Clara," said Earll. "It is so different from what was generally expected that we cannot make its contents public until we have questioned certain witnesses."

Earll put forth the rationale for his reluctance to divulge the contents of the letter. "We want them to tell the same story they would have told if the letter had not been found, and they would change their stories if they knew what was in the letter," Earll said. He indicated that the letter would be made public on Monday, when the coroner's inquest was resumed.

It was believed that the entire structure of the state's case might hinge upon this. Experts might be summoned to decipher the ink-written note. Further, the penciled message might force the student's father to tell on the witness stand whether the contemplated marriage mentioned in the note had been known to him and received his approbation. Otherwise, it would be regarded as a ruse by his son to induce Clara to flee home at midnight.

After the autopsy was completed, Clara's body was prepared for burial by the Otteson Funeral Home. The coffin was transported to the Chris Olson house late Saturday night. It was carried into the parlor of the rambling farmhouse around 11:00 PM. It was laid just below a photograph showing Clara in her confirmation class, a girl of 13 among other girls of "Little Norway."

More tidbits of news filtered out about the timeline of Clara's death and the finding of her body. The newly elected District Attorney, Arthur Curran, and newly elected Sheriff, Harry Underwood, believed that Clara Olson died between 12:30 and 1:00 on the morning of September 10.

The *Chicago Herald Examiner* reported, "Officials have come to the conviction that the slaying was done in an automobile; that a man sitting at the driver's wheel of a car could easily have obtained sufficient arm swing with a heavy, short hammer or similar object to inflict the fracture on the near or left side of the head of a passenger on the adjoining seat."

Erdman Olson's car was seized by Sheriff Sherwood. The Ford Roadster in which he and Clara took many rides through the countryside during their 18-month acquaintance showed evidence that it had been washed, with the new rubber matting in the bottom, fresh and clean. Yet long dark stains ran from the right-hand door of the car to the flooring. The stains were viewed by several newspapermen who swarmed over the vehicle.

Captain John Sullivan, private detective of Milwaukee employed by Clara's father, was inclined to doubt that anything worthwhile would be disclosed by analysis of the stains found on the inside of the right-side door, which some thought might be a deadly poisonous plant spray or other substance.

Authorities also released information that was sure to inflame the citizenry of Crawford County. It was also charged that the killer had robbed her. Clara's small purse, found with the body, was empty. Her father would state that she had at least $7 when she left, possibly more. The significance of the robbery, authorities believed, lay in the unverified report that the girl had been given money to carry out her elopement and that the money, as evidence of that, had been removed.

The buzz started to spread, arousing indignation and a deep sense of shame. In small groups gatherings after Sunday church services, at evening quilting bees, at the barbershop, and at the checkout counter of grocery stores, people could not stop talking about the discoveries. And the talk was not pleasant. "The son-of-a-bitch not only killed her, he robbed her." "What a low-life scum of the earth that young Olson is."

Searchers set out to brave the storm in an attempt to find the instrument the killer used to crush the girl's skull, along with her missing package of clothing. If Clara was going away for a few days, it was thought that she would be taking a suitcase or satchel or box of clothing. Searchers trudged to the desolate spot on Battle Ridge Knoll. There they found evidence that the body had been reclaimed from its wild resting place just in time, for wolf tracks led to the brink of the shallow pit.

Nearby, the household of Albert Olson, Erdman's father, still was quarantined because of scarlet fever that attacked Arvid Olson, Erdman's brother.

Reporters visited the Chris Olson farm instead. Arthur Olson, Clara's brother, who took a vow of revenge, was a Milwaukee electrical contractor, the only one of the large family to venture away from the Kickapoo Valley. He had taken complete charge in the emergency.

All of the sons and daughters feared their father would break down at the inquest. On Sunday, he walked aimlessly about the house, a milk pail on his arm. "I've got to help the boys milk," he answered to all the questions. He was troubled by the problem of how to get to the inquest, for snow and ice and high winds had made the roads virtually impassable for automobiles. He talked of using a horse and sleigh to reach the railroad ten miles away and board a train for Prairie du Chien.

Later, when the milk pail had been taken from him, he talked of his daughter. "I'm glad Clara is here," he said. "Instead of out in the cold woods in that heavy snow. Please don't talk to the women folks. They're all broken up. They cried all last night, and none of us slept. Emma [a daughter] was the worst. She yelled and we all ran downstairs. She thought she heard a man walking around the coffin, looking at Clara. We found nobody there."

Clara's mother, who could not cry when news of the discovery of her daughter's body first came, had finally obtained the relief of tears. "She cried last night," the father said. "And now Ma's all right again."

He also disclosed that some of his first prayers were not for his daughter, but for the youth he believed to be her killer, Erdman Olson. He reproved his son gently for his threat of revenge, saying, "Don't talk that way, Arthur, my boy. Erdman must have been crazy to do it. Your ma and me was prayin' all night for him."

Up at Gale College, President K. Lokengard declared that he knew nothing about the matter, and he saw nothing strange about the boy's action just before leaving college. "We have been pestered to death about this thing, but we don't know a thing about it. Of course, I am glad they have solved the mystery, but there seems to be no excuse for bring Gale College into the case as much as newspapers have been doing."

In the meantime, District Attorney Earll was following up on a rumor that Erdman had an accomplice. Did he have a companion with him when he drove to the home of Clara Olson and took her on a trip that ended in a shallow grave? Some people had seen a mysterious stranger that September 9 who got into Erdman's car. That was a mystery he planned to track down and solve.

Typical newspaper coverage of major events, such as the Clara Olson murder, a combination of story, photos, and sketches.

CHAPTER 14

The District Attorney Acts

Earll had spent all day Friday in the Rising Sun, Mt. Sterling, and Seneca areas questioning over 50 people. He carried a packet of subpoenas with him. In addition to following up on a rumored possible accomplice of Erdman Olson, Earll was seeking the girl with whom the student-Lothario had danced that fateful night. He wanted to know how the youth acted and what he said in those crucial hours leading up the murder.

Later that night, Earll released the names of those subpoenaed for the inquest: Chris Olson, aged father of the victim, his wife, their daughter Alice, son Bernard, and possibly other sons and daughters.

Among those for whom subpoenas were issued for the inquest were Andrew Helgerson and Oliver H. Helgerson, who accompanied Chris Olson to Gale College to confront Erdman and threaten his arrest, just a day before he suddenly disappeared.

Mr. Earll declined to say whether an arrest was imminent or whether a charge of perjury might be lodged against any person whose testimony was involved.

Chris Olson now told people, including reporters, about a second dream he'd had. In the new one, he related that he saw Clara lying face down in a shallow grave. The *Chicago Herald-Examiner* hired an expert on dreams, a Dr. Francis Gerty of Chicago's Cook County Hospital. He told the reporter, as printed in the December 4 issue, "I am afraid that the father so firmly believed he dreamed seeing the grave, rather than actually dreamed it. If he did, it was merely the reflection of the fear that had gone through his mind continuously. Freud's theory as to the stimulus which gives rise to dreams is that invariably it is found in the experience of the day before and has not been slept on. The dream itself is always elaborated on and represents the fulfillment of a wish or fear. Dreams, however have no prophetic value."

Nonetheless, the newspapers made a big deal out of Chris's dreams. One headline exclaimed:

FATHER'S DREAM OF GIRL IN GRAVE
CONVINCED HIM SHE HAD BEEN MURDERED

> Prairie du Chien, Wis (AP) The sinister dream of Chris Olson that his daughter Clara was dead had become reality.
>
> "I've seen Clara," the tobacco planter had declared long before the body of the pretty 22-year-old girl was found on in a shallow grave on Battle Ridge, near Rising Sun., a quarter of a mile from the home of Erdman Olson, who had been charged with the slaying. "I've seen her in a dream," Chris told neighbors. "I know she is dead. I saw her buried on her face on a hill near Rising Sun."

It should be noted, however, that his telling that he "saw Clara lying face down in a shallow grave" came after the discovery of his daughter's body. Some newspapers would write that he predicted exactly where the body would be found, but those details were divulged after the body was found, not before.

***

The newspapers were not alone in spreading false rumors. Sheriff Harry Sherwood had received a call late Thursday night from the sheriff of Dwight, Illinois. His departure, in view of the autopsy scheduled for Friday morning, was regarded as significant by reporters.

Sheriff Sherwood took the train to Dwight, Illinois, to interview a youth held there answering to the description of Erdman. The suspect gave his name as Walter M. Christensen, 22, and his home as Porter, Minnesota. The Dwight sheriff had sent a wire description of the youth held in his jail as that of Erdman Olson. Sheriff Sherwood declared the description corresponded with that of Erdman.

Yet when Sherwood visited the farmhand suspect in his jail cell, the young man claimed he was not Erdman Olson and maintained that he knew nothing of the case. In the flesh, Sherwood reported that Walter Christensen did not even resemble Erdman Olson. Christensen gave all a sheepish grin as he was released, along with a big sigh of relief, and prepared to go back to his corn husking in the neighborhood.

It would be the first of many false leads. A lad in Evansville, Wisconsin, was arrested. He gave his name variously as Paul Olstead, and also Williams. He would not divulge his nationality. Authorities released Olstead a few day later when authorities received a better description of Erdman.

A more substantial sighting caused great excitement in the hills and valleys of Crawford County. Authorities were certain they had located Erdman Olson. This news came out of Chicago.

Coroner Oscar Wolff on Saturday night expressed his conviction that the body of a youth in the county morgue there was that of Erdman Olson, sought for the slaying of Clara Olson of Prairie du Chien. Ignatius Sheehan, a police sergeant, said that the sheriff was fairly positive Friday night that the body was that of the accused youth. He was a suicide that had lain in the county morgue unclaimed since November 5.

"When I saw the picture of the missing youth," said Sheehan, "I was struck with the resemblance, and when I learned the body was slated for burial in the Potter's field, I obtained a stop order."

Sheriff Sherwood came down to view this body as well. He offered the belief that it was Olson, but he did not wish to take the responsibility of making a positive declaration of identification. Instead he wanted the father to see the body.

Adding fuel to the fire, Thomas Burke of 3145 North Central Park Avenue in Chicago also identified a young man in the morgue as Erdman Olson. After viewing the body, he told reporter, "I was born in Rising Sun, and I knew the Olson family all my life. They live right across the road from my uncle, Thomas Melvin. I have seen the Olson boys many times, but I haven't seen Erdman in six years. I am the night manager of the American Casket Company, and when there was a suggestion the boy in the county morgue was Olson, I told Louis Cohn, undertaker at 422 South Clark Street, that I knew Erdman, and I would go and see if I could identify the body."

Coroner Wolff asked Burke to call the Olson family in Wisconsin. They knew each other, and Burke told them the body was probably Erdman Olson, their son. The body appeared to be that of a man 10 years older than Erdman's 18 years, but that discrepancy was not deemed important. The man was about 5 feet 7 inches in height, weight 165 pounds, slim build, smooth face, light complexion, brown hair, blue eyes and a mole on the left thigh.

The claimed discovery ran aground, however, when the parents of the dead youth read about the description of the body in the morgue. They came over to view the body, and the youth's mother exclaimed, "He is my son, Charles." Her identification was made positive by a tiny scar on the left arm, the result of a burn suffered as a child.

The father of the dead youth, James Crowley, told newspaper reporters, "I own a drug store at 800 West 31st Street. I wanted my son to be a druggist. My wife and I were in Europe at the time the school season opened, and we thought when we returned that he had followed orders. When I found out the he hadn't, we quarreled. He left home on November 3, and I had not heard from him since."

Charles Crowley drank strychnine on November 5 and was found dead in the Tremont Hotel. The father claimed that his son hung around the drugstore quite a bit and knew the effects of poisons. Inconveniently for anyone wanting to identify him, the youth had registered under the name of John Carr.

Dr. John F. Crowley, dentist and uncle of the youth, examined gold fillings in the teeth. Dental records the next day confirmed the identification. Mervin Helgerson and Albert Olson, who were slated to go to Chicago to identify the body, instead remained in Wisconsin.

***

Sheriff Sherwood was in Chicago when he received word that another suspect was being held in Crawfordsville, Indiana. He requested that a picture of the youth being held be forwarded to Chicago. Sherwood evidenced interest in the Indiana suspect because he seemed to fit Olson's description in all items except weight. The Indiana suspect blinked his eyes rapidly and often, as did Olson.

Suspects in the Midwest—indeed, the entire nation—were arrested if they remotely fit the description sent out by authorities from Prairie du Chien. Many were released when the suspects did not meet the criteria of the description. Erdman had blue eyes, his tonsils had been removed, and he had a V-shaped scar under his right eye. Other characteristics, such as shifting weight from one leg to another and the constant blinking of eyes, seemed sufficient evidence for an arrest. The Indiana suspect was released after a few days.

Another report was printed about the Chicago police searching for Olson spurred by a man's report he had seen the boy in a restaurant. Nothing came of this lead.

Back in Prairie du Chien, District Attorney J. S. Earll had satisfied himself that when Olson went into the dance hall that fateful night, the grave in which Clara Olson's body was found was already waiting for her. He believed it was probable that plans were already laid for her "disappearance," and that all was in readiness when Olson dropped into the country dance for a moment to provide himself with an alibi. Why else would he have but one dance, then leave?

About 30 young people attended that Thursday night dance. Earll went to Seneca to question many of the young folks, hoping that someone might throw some light on the demeanor of Erdman

Olson. While he was there, he stated that he believed at least one other person besides Erdman knew the secret of her death.

Earll and members of the sheriff's staff ran down several other angles of the case. They discovered nothing, however, to throw new light either on the manner of the murder or the whereabouts of Erdman Olson, for whom a nationwide dragnet had been cast.

Earl also questioned Merle Murray, a farmer from Mt. Sterling. He stated that on that evening he met Erdman Olson at the Seneca dance, and he had taken a drink with him and a stranger at 11:30 PM, after which the youth and his companion departed together.

In addition, Earll talked to Park Morris, the proprietor of the Mt. Sterling hotel, who was at the same dance. He too saw Erdman and the stranger drive away in Erdman's car in the direction of Clara's farmstead.

The *LaCrosse Tribune* reported the following wrap-up of these efforts:

> Late Friday Earll returned from Mt. Sterling after interviewing Miss Marie Anderson, perhaps the last person to talk with the youth before the disappearance of Clara. Miss Anderson, and not her cousin, Christine Anderson, proved to be the girl with whom Erdman danced at the Seneca party, between 11 and 12 o'clock on the night of September 9. Earll questioned her closely about Erdman's actions and words at the time, but Miss Anderson could recall only that the youth seemed to have been in good spirits and apparently his usual self. He neither did not say anything unusual, she declared. He left the dance hall and drove away into the night immediately after dancing with her, she told the prosecutor.
>
> The state's theory is that Erdman showed up at the dance hall before going to the Chris Olson home for the purpose of establishing an alibi in case he should be questioned. Previously, it is believed, he must have chopped and dug his way through the matted tangle of roots in the oak clump on Battle Ridge, and prepared the grave to which Clara was to be taken.
>
> No additional light has been found on the report that an unknown male companion was with young Olson on the night

of September 9. The district attorney found no substantiation of the rumor that a man had remained in the car outside while Erdman went in to dance, and drove away with him afterward. However, he regards this angle of the case as of great importance and is still seeking substantiation, he said.

That the inquest will not get down to business until Monday seemed probable Saturday afternoon, as the authorities waited for Dr. Bunting to finish his gruesome business. Witnesses have been summoned and are here for the coroner's hearing, but it began to be apparent that little could be accomplished today beyond ascertaining if possible how the girl had died.

With the paucity of evidence, law enforcement authorities had to run down every possible lead. They would cast a wide net. For instance, Earll told reporters that there was a report from a banker in a village close to Great Falls, Montana. This informant said that sometime after Erdman Olson left Gale College on September 27, money was forwarded to him by his father through a Minneapolis bank. The district attorney planned to ask the father of the missing youth whether he had guilty knowledge of the fact his son had killed his sweetheart. After further investigation, authorities asked the sheriff in Great Fall, Montana, to check if Erdman had visited the home of Albert Severson. Anna Olson, his mother, was a Severson before she married Albert Olson in 1905.

In the same desperate vein, it was believed an appeal would be made to the Secretary of the Navy to institute a search throughout the service for the missing boy, who was said to have had, like most Scandinavians, an attachment for the sea. The exact information on which this belief of his enlistment was based could not be learned from officials, but it was said in this connection that a report, from a fairly authentic source, described Erdman's flight as taking him to the Northwest and the naval training and recruiting points on the West Coast.

How could the unsophisticated son of a tobacco farmer disappear so completely? That was the question that haunted the police over the ensuing weeks. It was hard to believe that he had dropped off the face of the earth.

The lane to the Olson farm shows the gate where Clara supposedly met Erdman for a midnight tryst in the early hours of Sept. 10, 1926.

CHAPTER 15

Two Families, Two Views

Rather than being possessed with an attitude of vengeance toward the slayer of the girl, the inhabitants of Prairie du Chien and scores of farmers visiting it since the body was removed from the grave on Battle Ridge hill were moved to a silence. A pall had spread over the length of the county.

This case astonished the remote countryside. Murder was practically unheard of in the hill country of southwest Wisconsin. Love leading to murder was a baffling outcome to these hardworking, thrifty farmers. Love meant marriage and children, happy and contented homes. The case of Clara Olson aroused the countryside as nothing before had ever done.

Groups gathered here and there on the streets and in various markets were talking in whispered tones, evincing no excitement over the partial solution of the mystery surrounding the disappearance and now the fate of Clara Olson. She had been found and the manner of her death disclosed. There was solace in knowing where she was and how she died. Two thoughts pervaded the countryside. First, give Clara a proper Christian funeral and burial, and second, seek out and find her killer. The people wanted justice.

In that regard, Justice Speck had been vindicated. He had taken a lot of heat when he issued a warrant on November 30 for the arrest of Erdman Olson on the complaint of Clara's father, when it was still uncertain that a murder had been committed. After the discovery of the body, he was now being portrayed as a hero by a sizable portion of Crawford County inhabitants.

They also saw the sense of Chris Olson, the bereaved father, insisting on the warrant. He knew, he had said, that his daughter was dead. And he was equally certain the Erdman Olson killed her. Yielding to his insistence, the authorities had issued the murder warrant, and organized the search party that stumbled across her body.

There were others who criticized Justice Speck and District Attorney Earll for waiting too long. Why did they not pursue this matter back on September 10 when Clara showed up missing? "They let the Olson boy have a seven-week head start," was a common complaint heard among the hill folks of Crawford County. This was a case of damned if you do, and damned if you don't.

Neither of the two Olson families had been visited by authorities since Friday afternoon, December 3, when District Attorney Earll went into the back country to endeavor to locate parties who had seen and danced with Erdman Olson at the Seneca pavilion on the night of September 9.

Nonetheless, the tide of public opinion had turned against the Albert Olson family. On Sunday, December 5, Albert, from his home in Rising Sun, attempted to call a lawyer in Prairie du Chien, He couldn't get through due to the winter storm. Both Olson families stayed at home from the Lutheran churches they attended that Sunday.

The city reporters who had gathered in the remote burg were not satisfied, however. Tidbits of news trickled out as those closest to Erdman Olson and Clara Olson were interviewed. The *Chicago Herald Examiner* interviewed Mervin Helgerson, 19, from Mt. Sterling. Mervin had known Erdman for three years, attended Mt. Sterling school as classmates, and "were pals." Helgerson was a classmate of Erdman's in the Mount Sterling School in 1922 and 1923. Helgerson says young men distrusted Erdman. Helgerson knew Clara through her employment on a neighbor's farm in 1924, where she worked as a maid for two months.

"We liked and trusted Clara a lot," young Helgerson said, "but we weren't so sure about Erdman. He was pretty much to himself, and nobody knew him very well."

As the inquiry progressed, additional light was thrown on the character of the youth who was the object of a nationwide search. One was the startling facts that emerged was that this was not the first time Erdman had killed somebody.

In July 1918, when he was age nine, he was exonerated in the death of a five-year-old boy, Charles Heavrin, with whom he was playing "wild west" or "war." The parents of both boys were at Soldiers Grove at the time of the incident. Reportedly, the Olson boy wanted to put some pep into their game and went into the house to retrieve a shotgun. He attempted to put a 16-gauge shell into a 12-gauge shotgun, however, and the shell exploded, striking Charlie Heavrin in the face, killing him instantly.

The country sheriff decided it was an accident, but some people thought it was Albert Olson, not the sheriff, who had decided that.

More information also emerged about his college years. In the *Galesville Republican*, it was reported that the Gale College authorities did not like the kind of advertising they had received from the daily press:

> Erdman Olson was little known to Galesville people and few town boys of his age were familiar with his name until the spotlight was thrown upon him.
>
> Gale college has had much undesirable publicity from the Olson case and while it is true that young Olson was a student at Gale, it is also true that he was expelled from that institution months before the tragedy and at the time he left the school, he was a student on probation."
>
> At college, Erdman Olson was not an intimate of any student. Neither boys nor girls held close association with him. While of a pleasing appearance, he had something about him that was repelling to other students. His disposition at times

was said to be anything but pleasant. On one occasion he attacked a student in a quarrel and knocked him out, whereby other college boys took him in hand. The student remained unconscious for four hours. He was bright, yet he was seldom up in his studies, and he did not apply himself.

The *Galesville Republican* further reported that early in 1925 a number of students participated in a disgraceful performance in the dormitories and were suspended. Olson is said to have been the leader. The faculty later reinstated the students, but Olson was allowed to return only on the pleas of his mother who asked that he be allowed another chance. Clara Olson never attended Gale College as reported by city newspapers.

Olson was fastidious in dress and the lad never lacked for funds. No accounts about town are reported against him, and his general deportment when off college campus has no bad marks, reported the newspaper.

A description of the alleged murderer is given out; Erdman Sanford Olson, murderer, is 18 years old. He weighs 165 pounds, is approximately 5 feet 7 or 8 inches tall, has light brown hair that may either be sleeked back or parted in the middle, has blue eyes, a light V shaped scar on the right side of his face.

The youthful college student has a habit of blinking his eyes continually and had a quizzical expression on his face. While a good mixer, he has a surly disposition and may be carrying a revolver. When young Olson fled, he was wearing a powder blue suit, a brown overcoat, light blue cap, oxblood shoes, size 8 or 8 1/2, It is believed likely, however, that he may change his clothing.

He had been thrown out of Gale College, once, then readmitted. He sang in the glee club, played baseball, and had a college sweetheart. Back home, he spent time with Clara. To his college acquaintance he referred to Clara as "my hick sweetie" or "the green country girl."

Student acquaintances at Gale College heard Erdman Olson say, "Offering me cows to marry his daughter. Them hicks must think I want to be one too!"

That Erdman Olson was just an ordinary college youth on the campus at Gale College during his two years there, but perhaps a little more "high-toned and possessed of plenty of spending money," was learned from people who knew him at Galesville today.

***

Despite the storm that Sunday, both Olson families were not averse to being interviewed by reporters. It meant they could get their side of the story out. Talking to newspapermen was also a method of finding out what was being reported—some new wrinkle, a bit of information, a message from someone. The two Olson families grilled visiting reporters in return, asking questions and getting information.

In the defense of his son, Albert Olson once again asserted it would have been impossible for the youth to make away with the girl, dig a shallow grave, bury her, and then reach his home by the time he did. Nor did he believe, he added, that Erdman could have tuned in the radio, talked with members of the family, and comported himself calmly if the blood of the girl was on his hands.

"And he would never have been crazy enough to dig a grave out on the open hillside to bury her if he had killed her," the father continued. "Hunters pass over that territory daily. It was certain the grave would be discovered. Erdman, had he done this thing, could have weighted the body and sunk it in the swamp on my own farm. It's the most desolate swamp in Wisconsin and nobody would every find a body in it."

He believed that the body of Clara was planted on the open hillside near his farm in order to cast suspicion on his son. "Erdman did not do it—I have proof that his clothes have not been mud stained."

In another interview, he contended that his son could not have had any direct part in the girl's disappearance. If Clara's father placed the time she left home between 1 and 2 AM, "Erdman came home that morning before 1:15," his father said. "He tuned in the radio, read for awhile, and by two o'clock was in bed. All the next day he helped us on the farm. And the next and the next. Then he went back to Gale college.

"Are these the acts of an 18-year-old boy guilty of murder? I haven't any idea where my boy is, but he isn't guilty of any crime. One of these days the girl will show up."

The *Chicago Herald Examiner*'s correspondent Harold L. Polland was holed up in Prairie du Chien that weekend. His job was to sell newspapers. They don't send newspaper reporters afield just to play tiddly winks. He talked often with both families. Both families were eager to tell their side of the story.

Albert Olson urged his son to come out of hiding and face charges that he murdered his 22-year-old sweetheart. "I know he is innocent. If only I could reach him, talk to him. I know he would return. I will spend any amount to prove that he did not commit any crime. I am trying harder than anybody, sheriffs and all, to locate him, and if I do, I will bring him home."

Albert Olson declared that his son had been the victim of coercion in an effort to make him marry Clara Olson and that he fled in alarm. "I haven't seen him or heard of him since he left school at Galesville, September 27," said Mr. Olson, denying reports that the youth had been communicating with him through an intermediary.

Reporters asked if reports attributed to Albert Olson that Clara Olson was alive in a maternity ward in St. Paul were true. He denied there was any basis for such reports.

Chris Olson was a sight with disheveled hair, ragged beard, and an old sheepskin duster that smelled of whiskey and hay. He told everyone he met, "I've seen her ... I know she's dead. I saw her buried on her face in a grave on a hill near Rising Sun."

In the meantime, as reported in the *LaCrosse Tribune* on December 4, Chris Olson was offering a reward. "And right there I made up my mind to follow this thing through," the old man declared. "I'll spend $10,000 if I have to just to get the man that killed my girl ..." Aged and bowed by his misfortune, he was certain that Erdman alone was responsible for the killing. And he intimated strongly that Albert Olson knew more than he was saying about the case. "Why, he came to me just two weeks ago and talked about Erdman and Clara," he said. "He told me: 'You'd better forget about all this and let Erdman alone. You'll get in trouble if you keep on.'"

Chris also recalled that Erdman's mother told him not to worry about Clara. She wasn't the only girl that had come home in the same condition and been at her wit's end about it. He told reporters, "Clara was not forced to leave my house. She was never told to go. We kept her in the fold. We would never put her out, and we were always willing to help her because Clara was always a good girl. She loved her home and her friends, and no matter where she is now, if she is alive, we want her to come back."

In addition, he related to reporters, that he, by himself, had visited Albert Olson farm a second time. The first visit on September 24, only Anna was at home. Chris recalls what Albert said to him on my visit to his farm in mid-November. Albert said, "Between me and you, you had better drop this thing." I said, "I won't drop it. I'll find that boy, and he'll tell me where the girl is if it costs me $1,000."

The lawyer Chris hired told him he thought Clara was probably dead. The private detective Chris hired, retired Madison detective Caswen, thought Erdman was probably staying with relatives, a grandmother in North Dakota or an aunt in Canada. Once Clara's body was found, the county sheriff and the DA sent telegrams to police in Milwaukee, Chicago, Minneapolis, and St. Louis. They also asked the Canadian Mounted Police to be on the lookout for Erdman.

The story of Chris's dream, coinciding with news of Clara's disappearance, death, and discovery, was rocketing east, west, and south to the biggest city newspapers in the Midwest. Chicago reporters and photographers began to converge on Prairie du Chien in earnest, the way searchers had gathered on Battle Ridge. Editors in the Windy City at the *Tribune* and *Daily News* trotted out a 1916 Wisconsin murder case, so sensational that made news even in the *New Your Times*.

The "Orpit murder case" had involved a pretty high school girl from Lake Forest, Illinois, and a pale, handsome college student from the University of Wisconsin. The girl believed she was pregnant, and the college boy was accused of poisoning her with cyanide. The body of the girl was found in a snowy clearing in a park in February 1916.

The boy's trial began in May and ended in July. Chemists, pathologists, and psychiatrists testified, sixty love letters were introduced as evidence, and friends and relatives testified about the girl's metal health. The boy told one intricate, foolish, and obvious lie after another.

News reports began from the day after the girl's body was discovered to the day after the jury delivered its verdict. The girl had killed herself with poison she had stolen from her high school chemistry lab. She wasn't pregnant but thought she was. She believed the boy planned to marry someone else. She had swallowed the poison after a final meeting with the boy in a park.

Now, ten years later, there was a new "pregnant girl/Wisconsin college boy" murder case. Had Clara really been pregnant? If so, maybe she had killed herself? Died after an abortion? Died because her college boyfriend thought she was nothing but a nuisance—a pregnant hick who needed a husband?

By now, newspaper readers in Chicago were beginning to know as much about Clara and Erdman as they'd once known about several local high-profile cases. Carl Wanderer was a murderer famous for what became known as "The Case of the Ragged Stranger." On June 21, 1920, Wanderer murdered his wife Ruth and a "ragged stranger" in a bizarre plot. His motivations were not totally known. It's believed the World War I hero became despondent when his wife became pregnant and he wanted to return to the Army. His wife opposed the move, so he shot her and a vagrant he hired to make it look like the couple were being robbed. There were many twists to this sad episode.

Cora Orthwein, divorced wife of a wealthy oil operator, shot and killed her former lover, Herbert Ziegler, district manager of the Goodyear Tire and Rubber Company. She was acquitted in March 1921. In the past 10 years, only two out of 16 women who killed men had been convicted.

Beulah May Annan, reportedly the "prettiest woman in Chicago," shot and killed her lover in April 1924. Beulah was acquitted on the third ballot. "Another pretty woman goes free," was the only comment made by Assistant State's Attorney William F. McLaughlin.

The June 6, 1924, issue of the *Chicago Tribune* ran this story: Belva Gaertner, another of those women who messed things up by adding a gun to her fondness for gin and men, was acquitted of the murder of Walter Law. "She was so drunk she didn't remember" whether she shot the man found dead in her sedan.

Harvey Church, age 21, was convicted of killing two car salesmen in 1922. Prison guards carried Church to the gallows after he went on a hunger strike. The newspapers recalled the most notorious Chicago homicides of the past. Now there was another sensational murder story "up there in Wisconsin," and they pulled out all the stops to tell the story and sell newspapers.

Going all out to sensationalize their coverage of the horrific crime, the *Herald-Examiner* hired a "character analyst and psychologist" who studied the bumps and lines on Erdman Olson's photo. They concluded: "In Erdman Olson we have a combination of aggressive-receptive type, the male quality of aggressive at times offsetting the feminine which is receptive. Consequently, a youth of this type would frequently get himself into trouble."

Meanwhile, feeding the local media frenzy, the detectives employed by Chris Olson told reporters that the girl was lured by a promise of marriage, taken to a lonely logging road, slain, and hastily buried by young Olson. Both John Sullivan and William Caswen were convinced of young Erdman Olson's guilt.

Chicago Herald Examiner staff correspondent Harry J. Romanoff managed to visit the Chris Olson household on that snowy Sunday, December 5. Chris Olson was milking his cows, and his wife was in the kitchen making breakfast when he reached the farmhouse. In one of the most poignant pieces on the case, the reporter captured the sorrow of that snowy morning:

In a chair by the kitchen window sat Alice, dry-eyed, quick fingered, sewing something white. "It's for Clara's funeral," she said simply. "It's a dress."

She did not mean she was going to wear white at the funeral of her sister. The dress was for the dead girl. I told them I had come to see Chris.

"Wait in there," said Chris' wife, turning from the stove and pointing to the open door of the parlor.

It was a bare little room, carpetless. An arm chair upholstered in black horsehair, a round table with a white cloth, a family album, in pink plush and three pictures on the walls were the room's equipment.

He came in from the barn, handed the foaming milk pail to "ma" and came to the parlor door. Like other members of the stoic family, he keeps his emotions deep hidden—unless you watch his eyes. They were filmy when I saw them. And once a tear escaped. Only once.

"You have news, news about Clara?" he asked me.

"It is not about Clara. It's only about the rumors one hears, rumors that perhaps you have some bits of knowledge not revealed," I asked.

"Why would I hide the truth?" he asks. "Truth is what I try to find. I want the truth—all of it."

"And revenge?" I suggested.

"I—I don't know" he said. "My faith has been in three things, the Bible is one, the law is another, and my family. Revenge—I don't know."

"That Erdman, he is bad. I begged him to take my best cows and horses and money and to marry Clara and live with her—just for a year. And he laughed at me. He is bad. He hurt my girl. He should be punished. But I do not want to hurt his father and his mother. You see?"

Then the old man paused to search his conscience.

"Maybe," he said. "I have been to blame. Maybe I have not been strict enough with my family. Maybe I should not have had Clara at home, not let her go to those parties at Seneca. Perhaps I am being punished for this."

The *Herald Examiner* reporter left the Chris Olson farmstead, venturing north on Highway 27 until he reached the Albert Olson farm. This father was far more definite in his opinions:

> Albert Olson, father of Erdman, young collegian, sought for the murder of Clara Olson, made the statement today, emphasizing the remark with a sweep of his arm over his rich 280-acre tobacco plantation.
>
> "Someone else killed Clara Olson," he added. "Erdman was a good boy and everyone called him a chip off the old block, and everything I have is behind him. To hell with the farm, to hell with everything! We can start over again, mother, Arvid, Erdman, and I. We are ready to go the rock-bottom limit for him because we have faith."

By that time drifting snow was piling high along the roads the farmer population must pass to reach Prairie du Chien for the Olson inquest starting on Monday morning. As the snow banks deepened, Sheriff Underwood feared many witnesses might have to risk their lives to give their testimony. Yet no one would miss the occasion, the most exciting inquest any had ever experienced in their lives.

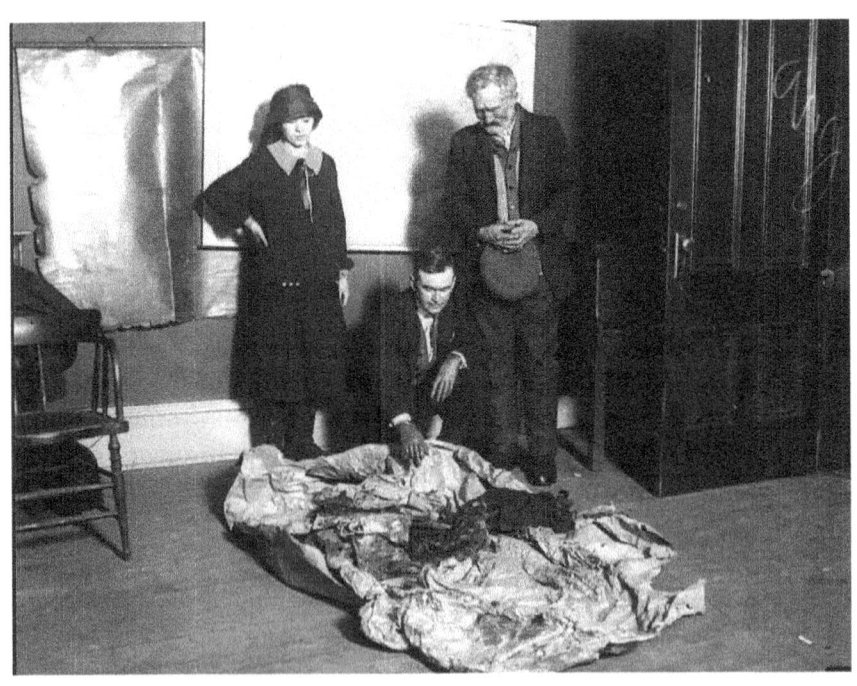

Chris Olson, right, views his daughter Clara's clothes Dec. 6, 1926, at an inquest into her slaying in Prairie du Chien. With Olson is daughter Alice, 19.

CHAPTER 16

The Pathologist Uncovers a Secret

The newspapers of the 1920s possessed one goal: sell newspapers. Lurid headlines were followed by grisly, shocking details rolled into heartrending stories to play on the emotions of the reader. The Sunday, December 5, City Edition of the *Chicago Herald Examiner* used the largest type set found in the press room. The headline, in bold 1.5-inch high letters, screamed: BLOW ON HEAD KILLED OLSON GIRL.

In the newsprint style of the era, there followed several sub-headlines, some of them wildly incorrect:

> MORGUE BODY IS IDENTIFIED AS ERDMAN'S
>
> Old Friend of Fugitive's Family Positive;
>
> Coroner Sending for Father to Confirm It
>
> Autopsy on Clara Discloses Triangular Skull Fracture;
>
> Inquest Opens Tomorrow

The newspapers matched the buzz going around Crawford County that Sunday. People had talked of nothing else since Clara's body was found. On farms, on tobacco tracts such as that owned by the youth's wealthy father Albert, in the woods of white oak and birch, where axes ring intermittently, on the streets of Seneca, Mt. Sterling, Gays Mills, all the tiny hamlets, people were talking of Clara Olson's death and asking how it was accomplished.

Some held that Clara was poisoned, and her body dumped in a shallow grave. One rumor had Clara drinking a toast to the wedding that would climax her adventurous midnight flight with her 18-year-old sweetheart, only to take a poison administered by Erdman Olson. Most tobacco farmers kept a supply of deadly nicotine to use as a spray on the tobacco corp. Nicotine sprays were a traditional remedy for a range of pests, including whiteflies, gnats, root and leaf aphids, thrips and leafminers. Half an ounce would be sufficient to cause death.

The formal inquest, with 15 scheduled witnesses, was to resume on Monday, December 6, presided over by Justice Speck, under the direction of Coroner Holly and District Attorney J. S. Earll, assisted by District Attorney–elect Arthur Curran. Earll had indicated he would like to "get the inquest done in one day." The funeral for Clara Olson is set for the next day, and the weather looked very bad. A winter storm was blowing in from the north and west. Members of both Olson families have been summoned. Sheriff deputies had gone into the hills around Seneca, Mt. Sterling, and Rising Sun on Friday December 3 to secure witnesses.

Five hundred people came to the courthouse in Prairie du Chien. They arrived in cars, wagons, buckboards, buggies, and sleighs. Farm folks from 50 miles around trekked through a blizzard. It was the most dramatic event since the first settlement, a fur trading post, was established here in Revolutionary days.

Nor were they all natives of the purple hills. Automobiles were bringing hundreds from every direction, from across the Mississippi River in Iowa and Minnesota and from all parts of Wisconsin. They were waiting to hear what Dr. Bunting found when the clay and mud was scraped away from Clara's body.

Dozens of newsmen, reporters from major newspapers, had been making Prairie du Chien their temporary home as they gathered information for the latest story to relay back to their newspapers, including R. L. Bangsberg from the *La Crosse Tribune and Leader Press*, Harold L. Polland from *Chicago Herald-Examiner*, and Orville Dwyer from the *Chicago Daily Tribune*.

Great precautions were taken in conducting the inquest. Witnesses were kept out of the courtroom, and called one at a time, and when each witness was finished, he was sent from the room before the next took the stand. In the anteroom they were closely guarded by deputies who permitted no one to talk to them.

District Attorney Earll had a list of 15 people he wanted to testify, including Albert and Anna Olson; Chris Olson, the hired man; Edwin Knutson; Erdman dance partners, Marie Anderson and Christine Anderson; Clara Olson's brother Bernard, her sister Alice; Andrew Helgeson; Charles Bown; James Nederloe; Ernest Otteson; farmer Merle Murray; and Park Morris, proprietor of Mt. Sterling Hotel. Earll would take his turn as well, scheduled to be the last to take the stand.

Albert Olson was the first to be called. Accounts by two different newspapers highlighted how reporters perceived the same event. The first account stated, "The father on the stand was calm and cool. He answered all questions adequately and promptly, and volunteered very little except in answer to the interrogations of District Attorney J. S. Earll."

The second journalist reported another man entirely: "Albert was nervous, evasive, and hesitant. He gulped and his eyes shifted. He started his testimony in a husky whisper, so low one could not hear him 10 feet away. Albert had been calm and collected. He lost all that on the stand."

During his examination, Earll apparently was attempting to discover if, as reported, he had threatened Chris Olson if he did not drop the inquiry that led up to the discovery of the girl's body. Earll also wanted to know if he had been in communication with his son since he disappeared.

There were a number of preliminary, factual questions. Where do you live, Mr. Olson? How long have you lived there? What is your occupation? The fact that Clara Olson had written him a letter last summer, in which she asked him to make Erdman marry her, was one of the high spots of the testimony. Olson said he had sent Erdman over to the girl's home to demand a medical examination and "fix it up." The boy had returned and reported he had done nothing. His testimony included his response when Chris Olson, the girl's father, had visited Gale College to confront Erdman about the whereabouts of his daughter. Then, he said, he had visited the girl's family for the first time, suggesting that if they would let matters alone, the girl would come back, and everything "would be all right."

Then Earll asked Olson about the night of the murder.

Q. Do you recall where you were on the 9th of September last?
A. Yes, sir.
Q. Where were you? Home all day?
A. Yes, sir.
Q. What members of your family were there at your home on that day?
A. They were all there.
Q. Is there anyone in your family besides those above named?
A. Our hired man, Ed Knutson.
Q. Was he there also on that day?
A. Yes, sir.
Q. Were you all there that day?
A. Yes, sir. Until evening.
Q. Till what time in the evening?
A. Eight o'clock, perhaps.
Q. Were you away after that?
A. Yes, sir.
Q. Who was with you?
A. Albert Malone.
Q. Were all the other members of our family home when you left?
A. Yes, sir. Knutson had gone before I left.
Q. The hired man had gone before you left. But your wife and your sons were there.

A. Yes, sir.
Q. What time did you get back?
A. Between 10 and 11 that evening.
Q. Who was there when you returned?
A. My wife and my little boy.
Q. Erdman was away at that time?
A. Yes, sir.
Q. Do you know where he was?
A. I know where he said he was going.
Q. Where did he say he was going?
A. Seneca to the dance.
Q. What time did you retire?
A. Right around 11, shortly before 11, I think.
Q. Did the rest of the family retire at that time?
A. They had gone to bed before that.
Q. Did Erdman come home that night?
A. Yes, sir.
Q. Do you know what time?
A. I don't know exactly.
Q. Do you know about when?
A. About a quarter past one.
Q. How do you fix that time?
A. Well, he said himself it was a quarter past one. My wife knows about what time he came home.
Q. Did you hear him when he came in?
A. I did.
Q. You didn't look to see what time it was.
A. I didn't.
Q. What, if anything, did he do after he came home?
A. That I don't know.
Q. You don't know whether he did anything or not?
A. No, I don't.
Q. What did you do on the 10th of September?
A. Harvested tobacco.
Q. Were you home that day, all day?
A. Yes, sir.
Q. Who else was there?
A. The members of the family.

Q. All of them?
A. Yes, sir.
Q. And your hired man?
A. Yes, sir.
Q. And on the 11th?
A. Harvested tobacco.
Q. You were there on that day?
A. Yes, sir.
Q. Are all the members of the family with you now?
A. No, sir.
Q. Which one is gone?
A. Erdman.
Q. When did he leave?
A. The 12th of September.
Q. What day of the week was that?
A. Sunday.
Q. And about what time of day did he leave?
A. About half past eight o'clock.
Q. Where did he go?
A. To Galesville.
Q. How did he go?
A. By car.
Q. Did you take him?
A. No, sir.
Q. Who did take him?
A. Knutson, the hired man.
Q. You say that Knutson had left home on the night of the ninth before you had?
A. I think so.
Q. When after the 12th of September did you see your son, Erdman?
A. I haven't seen him since.
Q. Do you think that you heard from him inside of seven days from the time he left on the 12th?
A. Yes, sir.
Q. You had a letter from him?
A. Yes, sir.
Q. When after that?

A. On the 27th, I believe.

Q. Did you get the letter on the 27th, or was it written on the 27th?

A. I believe it was written on the 27th from Galesville.

Q. Do you recall the contents of that letter or do you have the letter?

A. No, sir.

Q. Alright, you may state as nearly as you can recall what he said in that letter.

A. Well, he said he was leaving Galesville, because Mr. Olson had been up there and threatened him.

Q. You mean Chris Olson?

A. Yes, sir. He said he told Chris he didn't know anything about her whereabouts, but thought she was in St. Paul, and that he would have a few days to get her back, so he could do something for himself and get away.

Q. So he could get away?

A. Yes, sir.

Q. Did he say anything that would indicate that he might possibly take his own life?

A. Yes. I think he did.

Q. Did he say something to the effect that while life was sweet, he would prefer to taking his own life rather than be caught, or words to that effect?

A. I think so, something similar.

Q. Well, when after the reception of this letter did you hear from him again?

A. I haven't heard from him since.

Q. Have you seen any letter that was written to anyone else?

A. No, sir.

Q. Have you done any communication with him since that time?

A. No, sir.

Q. Do you know how much money he had when he left home on the 12th of September?

A. I gave him $20.

Q. Do you know how much he had when you gave him that $20?
A. Perhaps $6 or $7.
Q. No more than that?
A. I don't think so.
Q. How much money have you sent him since he left home?
A. $40.
Q. When did you send him the $40?
A. I didn't send it to him. He wrote checks on the bank.
Q. Did he write checks on the bank of Gays Mills?
A. Two checks, one was $25, and one was $15.
Q. Do you know when those checks reached the bank of Gays Mills?
A. Possibly a week or ten days later.
Q. Do you know where those checks were written?
A. At Galesville.
Q. Has he cashed any other checks on your account in any other bank?
A. Not since he left on this last time.
Q. Do you know what automobile Erdman had when he went to the dance at Seneca?
A. Yes, sir, his own, a Ford roadster.
Q. You have two automobiles; what is the other one?
A. Ford, too.
Q. Is that the same car that was used by Knutson when he took the boy to Gale college?
A. Yes.
Q. Are you acquainted with the Chris Olson family?
A. Three members.
Q. Which ones?
A. Chris, Bernard, and I forget the other fellow's name.
Q. The other boy?
A. Yes, sir.
Q. How long have you known them?
A. About two months and a half.

Q. Do you recall the circumstances of the beginning of your acquaintanceship with them? Where did you first meet them?
A. On their place.
Q. You went to their place?
A. Yes, sir.
Q. What was the occasion for your going to their place at that time?
A. I wanted an explanation for his trip to Galesville.
Q. And your trip to the Chris Olson place was occasioned by the contents of your letter from Erdman which he wrote you after Chris Olson had been to see him at Galesville. Was that right?
A. Yes, sir.
Q. Well, do you recall the conversation that you had with Mr. Olson?
A. I recall that he claimed that my boy took the girl away.
Q. On the night of the 9th or the morning of the 10th?
A. Yes, I guess so.
Q. He said she went away between twelve and one o'clock. Do you recall anything else that was said in that conversation?
A. He said he saw car lights drive up to the gate and turn around, and he believed he seen another car in the road at that same time. He offered my boy property and money to go and get the girl and marry her.
Q. Was this the first conversation you had had either with Chris or any of the boys after the ninth?
A. The first conversation I have had with Chris, yes.
Q. But you have had a conversation with Chris or any of the boys at that time.
A. Yes, sir.
Q. What was the date of that conversation?
A. The morning of the tenth.

Q. The next morning after the Seneca dance?
A. Yes, sir.
Q. Which one of the boys did you talk with at that time?
A. Bernard.
Q. Where did you have that conversation?
A. At my place.
Q. What time of the day?
A. About six o'clock in the morning.
Q. What was the conversation you had with Bernard that morning?
A. He told me he was looking for his sister, but he didn't have a search warrant.
Q. Yes, what else?
A. He told me his sister left between one and two o'clock in the night. He told me he had tracked the car from their gate out to 27 and that the car that turned around has got an odd tire.
Q. Your car didn't have an odd tire did it?
A. No, sir.
Q. Is that all the conversation you had that you told us?
A. Oh, he told me some dog stories and such stuff outside. A little conversation I couldn't remember in detail.
Q. When did you next have conversation with Chris Olson or his boys?
A. The evening that I mentioned that he drove down once since afterwards.
Q. Do you recall the substance of that conversation?
A. Not exactly.
Q. What was the conversation?
A. Mostly about where they might possibly be.
Q. Did you make any suggestion either you or your wife about letting the matter rest that matters might clear themselves up later?
A. Possibly we did.

Q. Don't you know you did, or words spoken to that effect?
A. Yes, sir.
Q. Did you make any suggestions of holiday time or the first of the year?
A. I believe I did.
Q. Was there something said in that conversation to the effect that the girl had been taken away to give birth to a child and that after the child was born she would return.
A. We spoke about possibilities.
Q. You don't know whether he had any knowledge of her whereabouts?
A. No, sir.
Q. Had you had any talk with your boy in reference to this?
A. Yes, sir, about the middle of August. I sent him down there.
Q. You sent him down there? Why?
A. Because she wrote me a letter.
Q. She wrote you a letter? What about?
A. She wanted my boy to marry her because she was in a family way.
Q. You sent the boy down there? What did you do?
A. I instructed him to bring her up to our place.
Q. Did she come?
A. No, sir.
Q. Did you ever see her?
A. No, sir.
Q. You don't remember the date mark of that letter?
A. The 17th of August.
Q. Will you produce it for the record?
A. Yes, sir.
Q. Did you have any further conversation with the boy about the girl before he went away to school?
A. I asked him that night what was done. He said nothing.

Q. You don't mean to tell me that you didn't have any further talk with him before he went away to school in regard to this?
A. I can remember I asked him once whether he heard anything from this girl and he said "No."
Q. Do you recall him writing a letter about the 6th of September, two or three days before the dance at Seneca?
A. I don't know.
Q. Where did he do this writing?
A. Generally on the dining room table. Sometimes I mailed his letters.
Q. Who were Erdman's close associates?
A. He chummed with Oscar Peterson, Oscar Mickelson, and a cousin, Walter Severson, and corresponded with Oscar Halstad, of Coon Valley.
Q. Referring to the talk you and your wife had with Chris, did you tell him to go home and forget this case and that girl would come home with her child?
A. I did not say exactly that. I tried to cheer him up. I told him that the girl would be home.

Albert Olson did not volunteer information beyond the curt answers to questions posed by District Attorney Earll. Newspaper accounts stated that Olson appeared a bit subdued and spoke in a low voice at the beginning of his testimony but seemed more assured and confident as the questioning continued. It was clear from Albert Olson's tone and demeanor that he was convinced his son had nothing to do with Clara's disappearance and murder.

ESTABLISHED 1837. NO. 33,487. TUESDAY MORNING, DECEMBER 7, 1926 Price 3 Cents EIGHTEEN PAGES—TWO SECTIONS

CORONER'S INQUEST NAMES ERDMAN OLSON MURDERER

| WETS WHET AX | "Happy It's Over" | RICH FLORIST | BLAINE'S LAST | 'Keep Mum,' Boy | JURY REACHES

(Top) *Anna Olson testifies and angerly defends her accused son.*
(Bottom) *Edwin Knutson, hired hand on the Albert Olson farm, was grilled by the District Attorney on the witness stand and later.*

CHAPTER 17

The Questioning Continues

Anna Olson was the second person called to the witness stand. Newspapers reported that she was nervous when she took the stand but collected herself after answering a few questions and maintained a steady composure. Her voice broke a little when she recited, almost word for word, the last letter received from her son in which he said he would not be seen again "except in a coffin." Apparently, after reading it so many times, she had memorized the letter by heart.

Her voice shook a little again as she declared her confidence that Erdman had not committed suicide. "He wouldn't kill himself," she asserted with a ring of assurance.

Erdman, she asserted "had left to get away from all this mud." She clearly put the blame for her son's disappearance on Clara's father. She defiantly declared, "Chris Olson threatened him with everything under the sun."

It was the typical example of an aroused mother's love, refusing to believe anything negative about her firstborn, regardless of his plight or the numbers of appearances against him.

Her testimony at the coroner's inquest into the death of Clara Olson went as follows:

Q. Where were you on the night of September 9?
A. At home.

Q. Do you recall anything about a dance at Seneca your son Erdman attended that night?
A. Yes.
Q. Do you know what you were doing at that time?
A. The usual housework.
Q. Who was there?
A. Just the family.
Q. Where was your husband?
A. At Fairview
Q. When did he return?
A. About 10:30
Q. Had you all retired?
A. Yes
Q. What time did Erdman get home?
A. About 1:15.
Q. What do you fix that time by?
A. By the time he had been downstairs before the time he was in bed and the clock struck 2.
Q. Did he tune in on the radio that night?
A. I don't know, but I thought I heard the ear phone.
Q. Did he eat a lunch?
A. Well, there were crumbs and signs of lunching.
Q. Did he have a visitor in the morning?
A. Yes, sir.
Q. Who was it?
A. An Olson boy. I don't know his name.
Q. Did he come in?
A. No, he called Erdman out to him.
Q. You didn't hear them?
A. Yes, I did. He asked him if he went away that night.
Q. What did he say?
A. He said he was away.
Q. That was the conversation between your son, Erdman, and Chris Olson's son?
A. He told Clara had left.
Q. Anything else?
A. He asked to see the car. Then Erdman asked what time of night she left, and her brother said between

one and two. Erdman said he was home at that time.
Q. Where was this conversation?
A. Right outside the kitchen door.
Q. Did Erdman tell him he hadn't seen Clara the night before?
A. I didn't say that.
Q. Did he say he knew where she was?
A. He said that he hadn't taken her away.
Q. Do you know where your son had been the night before?
A. I know where he said he was going.
Q. Where was that?
A. To Seneca to the dance.
Q. Did he mention seeing anyone?
A. Yes.
Q. Who?
A. He said something about Johnny Dolan and Arlene. And he said the music was very good.
Q. Are you acquainted with the Chris Olson family?
A. I have known them since this trouble came.
Q. Before your son left home to go to school on the 12th of September, do you know anything about his relations with Clara Olson?
A. Yes.
Q. What do you know about them?
A. We received a letter from her in August.
Q. What did she tell?
A. She said she wanted Erdman to come down to get married.
Q. What else did she say?
A. She didn't want her folks to know about it. She didn't want to put Erdman in trouble.
Q. What else?
A. She said in four-and-one-half months she was expecting a child.
Q. Did she say anything about who was the father of the child?

A. No.
Q. Erdman wasn't surprised, was he?
A. He said he knew about it, but he wasn't at home at that time.
Q. He went down?
A. He went down, and we sent word that we wanted to speak to her, and she refused to see us.
Q. You never knew this girl?
A. I never knew her to speak to.
Q. You didn't go to see her yourself?
A. No. I didn't, because she didn't want her folks to know, and we didn't feel the boy was guilty. The boy said he asked her for a doctor's examination, and she refused it.
Q. You didn't suggest marrying the girl if he was responsible?
A. We said he would have his choice, as we know the law couldn't compel him to.
Q. Was that all the conversation you have about the girl from the time the letter was shown and the time he came back?
A. I asked him from time to time if he had heard about it or if she had dropped the case. He said at one time she had.
Q. When was that?
A. About the 18th of last August.
Q. You got the letter about the 19th?
A. Yes
Q. And he told you she had dropped it?
A. Yes, because her time did not correspond with the time he was back from school.
Q. He went to dances, to the store, the same as other boys did in the evening?
A; Yes.
Q. He often got in at 12 or 1 o'clock?
A. Yes.
Q. After you received that letter you had some conversation with Chris Olson, didn't you?

A. Yes.
Q. After your boy had left Gale College?
A. Yes, sir.
Q. And a long time after the girl has been missed first.
A. It couldn't have been over four weeks.
Q. What was that conversation?
A. He asked if the boy had returned, or if we had heard from him.
Q. What did you tell him?
A. We hadn't.
Q. What else did he talk about?
A. Well, he had men up to Galesville to make inquiries. He said he had heard that Erdman had rolls of money. I told him that wasn't so.

Anna remained calm on the stand, speaking in a low voice that could barely be heard. Several times she was admonished to speak louder. Her voice broke once, when she was asked if she had seen her son since Erdman returned to Gale College.

Anna Olson tried in vain to keep the letter from Clara to herself.

"You have that letter? Mr. Earll asked.

"Yes" she replied.

"Will you bring it here?" he asked.

"Yes, if I can find it," she quickly replied.

"Then bring it here tomorrow," Mr. Earll retorted in a stern voice.

Justice Speck ordered that Anna turn over the letter she and her husband, Albert, had received from Clara Olson. Newspapers report that Anna seemed defensive and defiant.

Anna Olson related that after their son returned to school about September 20, he asked in his first letter home, "Has the party who made its disappearance come back?"

In a second letter to the mother, he asked that his parents send his clothes and described himself as "very busy." In his third and last letter, he said Clara's father and "visitors" had been to see him. The contents of this letter had already been made public. It was the last letter Erdman sent to his folks.

Edwin Knutson on the Stand

The Olsons' farm hand was on the stand at the end of the noon recess, testifying to his own and Erdman's movements on the night of the girl's disappearance. Knutson appeared very nervous and fidgety and shifted back and forth in the witness chair.

District Attorney Earll called for a recess at 12 noon for a lunch period. Justice Speck agreed. Knutson was to be questioned further in the afternoon. Earll talked briefly to reporters during the noontime break. The mysterious contents of the letter found in the girl's bosom when pathologists examined her body on the Saturday, the letter which Earll declared put the whole case in a new light is "highly sensational," was not revealed during the morning session. Earll indicated he might get to that letter and its contents during the afternoon. At least a dozen witnesses remain to be questioned.

The reopening of testimony scheduled at two o'clock was delayed until close to three by the private questioning of witnesses, mainly on the Chris Olson side of the case, by District Attorney J. S. Earll.

Edwin Knutson was returned to the stand when the hearing eventually reopened.

Q. Do you know Clara Olson?
A. Yes, I have known her for four or five years.
Q. Were you present when Bernard Olson came to the Albert Olson farm on the morning of September 10?
A. Yes.
Q. Do you know where Erdman Olson was on the night of September 9?
A. I do not know.
Q. Was Erdman in the habit of going out evenings?
A. Yes.
Q. Did you know he was going with Clara Olson?
A. Yes.
Q. Did you drive Erdman to Galesville when to returned to school?

A. Yes
Q. What mention was made of Clara Olson during your trip to Galesville together?
A. Clara Olson's name was not mentioned on the trip.
Q. Do you mean to say the name of Clara Olson was not mentioned on the trip?
A. No.
Q. What was the conversation?
A. Mostly about school.
Q. Have you told all you know about this case?
A. Yes, I have.

Chris Olson Takes the Stand

Reporters on hand were ready to telephone their story to their headquarters in Chicago, Milwaukee, La Crosse, Winona. The next day *Chicago Herald-Examiner* and *Chicago Daily Tribune* December 7 issues devoted several pages to the crime and the inquest that had taken place the previous day.

The following is a brief excerpt of Chris Olson taking the stand in the morning session. He was dressed in a dark brown coat and an odd pair of trousers, a checkered sweater coat and checkered shirt, without a tie and hair unkempt. He seemed about to collapse."

Q. Where do you live, Mr. Olson?
A. About three miles northwest of Seneca, I think.
Q. In what town?
A. Town of Seneca.
Q. How long have you lived there?
A. I have been on that place out there about 30 years
Q. You have a family? You may give the number.
A. There is 5 girls and 4 boys now.
Q. You have a wife?
A. Yes.
Q. What are the names of your boys?

A. Bernard, Arthur, and Adolph.
Q. And you have some daughters. What are their names?
A. Minnie, Ella, Alice.

The old man's head fell on his hands and he seemed about to faint. He sat with his shoulders heaving for two or three minutes, while windows were hurriedly thrown open to let in fresh air. District Attorney–elect Arthur Curran patted the aged man on the back and tried to comfort him. "I can't name her!" sobbed Chris finally. The questioning continued.

A. Minnie, Emma, Cornelia.
Q. Was one named Alice?
A. Yes.
Q. And there was another?
A. Inga.
Q. And you had a daughter Clara?
A. Yes.
Q. What were you doing on the night of September 9th?
A. Oh, I was up and looked out a couple of times between 10 and 12 o'clock.
Q. Did Clara go out any time that night that you know of?
A. Just about 12 o'clock at night time.
Q. About 12 o'clock by your time.
A. Yes, it was five minutes to 12:00 when I blowed out the lantern, and she went out just about a couple of minutes after I went to bed.
Q. How did you know it was Clara going out at that time?
A. I asked who it was and she came down from upstairs and she said it was "Clara."
Q. Did you see her again after that?
A. No. I didn't see any person, but I saw a car. There was a car coming down the road past my neighbor, Mr. Crowley's place, and when I blew out the lantern.

Q. How far, Mr. Olson, is that from the road that turns into your place?
A. About a hundred yards, I think.
Q. Your house isn't right on the road, is it?
A. It is 80 rods from the highway.
Q. Did you watch that car?
A. Yes, I looked through my front door through the glass, and I saw him turn around, this way, between me and my neighbors on the other side. Turn right close, and turned this way, and the light went out.
Q. Where were you at the time you saw that?
A. Looking through my front door after I blew out the lantern.
Q. Did Clara come that night?
A. She hadn't. Well, I had a dream; that is the reason I woke up. That was between 1 and 2. I don't know exactly what time I got up, but it was between 1 and 2.
Q. Did you make any investigation the next morning in regard to that car that came up the road and turned around there in front of your place?
A. Yes, I told the boys to go over and look at the track, what kind of track it was.
Q. Did you look at them yourself?
A. No.
Q. Did you know Erdman at the time?"
A. I knew who he was but never had a talk with him.
Q. When after that did you go see him?
A. Up at Galesville College, September 26.
Q. Did anyone go up there with you?
A. Andrew Helgerson and Oliver Helgerson.
Q. Did you see Erdman then?
A. Yes.
Q. What conversation did you have with him?
A. I asked him what time he had made up his mind to go back to college, and he said, "I don't hardly know you."

Q. And what was the conversation?
A. I asked him if he had seen Clara.
Q. And what did he say?
A. He said no. He also said he did not call for her on the night of September 9, but I can prove the man who took my daughter away was Erdman Olson.
Q. What did Erdman say about that?
A. He said I couldn't prove a thing and went down the street with a couple of other boys on the campus.
Q. What else did you say?
A. I told him he was the man who ordered Clara to burn all of her letters that day. I told him Alice had seen Clara burn the letters.
Q. What else happened?
A. Well, I put my arm around Erdman's shoulder and told him I wanted to talk to him. "You wrote the letter and told Clara to meet you, didn't you?" Mr. Olson testified he said to Erdman.
"If you denied seeing her that night, who did take her away, Chris Olson asked the boy, his testimony showed."
Q. Well, what did you ask him next?
A. What he did with Clara on 9th of September.
Q. And what did he say to that?
A. He said he hadn't seen her.
Q. What next did you ask him?
A. He said he never went down and got her. I told him I can prove it. He said, "You can't prove nothing on me," and then started to go away.
Q. What did you say next?
A. I only said, "You gave that girl instructions to burn your letters. Sometimes she missed the wrong one," and he turned around, and got kind of weak. He asked me if I saw the letter.
Q. What did you say?
A. I said, "Alice saw it." He asked me if his name was on there.
Q. And what did he say to that?

A. I said it didn't make any difference when you own up you wrote the letter.

Q. Did he own up he wrote it?

A. Yes, he owned up to that before, he said he told Bernard, too, he wrote the letter the next morning.

Q. What further talk did you have?

A. Well, I waited ten minutes, and then I put my hand on his shoulder, and "Erdman, I want to talk just a few minutes to you," I said, "Before I go home. Erdman, you own up you wrote the letter. You told her in that letter to meet you at the door at 12 o'clock, didn't you?"

Q. What did he say?

A. He said, "I did."

Q. And then what did you say to him?

A. I said, "You denied you saw her that night and if you didn't, you sent somebody else to take her, because you called her out to the road," and he said he took her to Viroqua. I said, "I don't believe it because I saw the tracks the next morning, and they were from the south."

Q. What did he say to that?

A. He said he turned around and came back. I asked him where she went to, and he said St. Paul.

Q. Did he tell you how she was to get to St. Paul?

A. I told him I didn't believe the girl had very much money, and he said he gave her $20.

Q. Anything else?

A. I told him I didn't have any strings on the girl. She was of age, and all I asked was that she would write a few lines so we can see whether she was alive. He said he couldn't do that. I said, "Erdman, is there anything between you and the girl that we don't know anything about? If you bring her back, I will help you all I can." He didn't answer me.

Olson went on to testify that he gave Erdman until Thursday of that week to bring Clara back, and warned him that if the girl did not show up, he would send the sheriff for him. "There is something wrong if Clara does not show up," Mr. Olson said.

Q. Did you hear from him later?
A. I got a letter the next day.
Q. Where's the letter?
A. I haven't it. Caswen has it.
Q. What did the letter say, as you recall?
A. Erdman wrote it was his business where the girl was at the present time, that she would be back when he came back, and admitted that he lied about the girl going to St. Paul.
Q. Did you know Erdman's father and mother before this?
A. No.
Q. Did you ever talk with them?
A. They came to my house after they got a letter from him.
Q. What was the conversation?
A. They told me I made a big mistake going to Galesville and scaring the boy away from school.
Q. What else went on?
A. I told them I had received a letter from Erdman, and Albert Olson wanted to see it, but I wouldn't let him. They talked at this time about the story printed in the *La Crosse Tribune* soon after the disappearance.
Q. Did Albert Olson have the *Tribune* with him?
A. Yes.
Q. What was said?
A. Olson showed me the paper and asked me if I had anything to do with that story.
Q. What did you say?
A. I told him I have not set foot inside the city of La Crosse for 10 years, except when I went through to Galesville.
Q. What else was in the conversation.
A. Albert said that we better drop the investigation.

Q. What did you say to that?

A. I said no. I will find the boy who took Clara away if it cost me $1,000. Albert said Erdman did not have to tell where the girl was. He said I was a fool to start the investigation.

Q. What else did you say?

A. I told Albert that Clara went away without enough clothes, and Albert said she had plenty of clothes.

Q. Have you told all of the conversation?

A. I told him, "Now you go down to the car and tell them, Oliver Helgerson and Andrew Helgerson, what you told me." He went down and told them the same thing.

Q. What there any further talk that you recall?

A. Well, I don't remember any more at that time. But his dad came back the same day the article came in the *La Crosse Tribune* stating my daughter was missing. He pulled out the paper and asked me if I knew anything about it. He said, "Between me and you, you had better drop this thing." I said, "I won't drop it. I'll find that boy and he'll tell me where the girl is, if it cost me $1,000. He said you can't find him, and that I was foolish in the first place to say anything about it. I said that the girl went away with no clothes and he said she had enough clothes.

Q. Anything else at that time?

A. No. Later I went to his house and I asked Albert Olson what he would do, and he said let it go for a while. His wife said something I will remember as long as I live. It was, "It would be like a lot of other girls. She would be home after New Year's with a baby without any man." That's the first time we knew anything about it.

Q. At that time you knew nothing about your daughter being in trouble?

A. Not a bit, not anyone in our family.

Q. What day of the week was this, Mr. Olson?

A. Sunday.

Q. When next did you see the Albert Olsons?
A. Well, they came back to my place about the middle of the week, Wednesday or Thursday evening. I don't know but either one or the two.
Q. Shortly after you came back from Galesville?
A. The day after I received the letter. Well, they came there and told me I made a bad mistake when I went up to Gale College to scare him out of school. They said they received a letter that came from him. Then I told him I had a letter the same day.

By early afternoon, the major players in the Clara Olson murder inquest had testified: Albert and Anna Olson, their hired man, Ed Knutson, and Chris Olson, bereaved father of Clara.

What came out in the testimony that had not previously been reported? Nothing startling. Timelines of events were established. Nuances were brought forth. For example, both parents of Erdman Olson were extremely defensive of their son. They wanted to tell the world their son could not carry out such a hideous murder. The fact that the letter from Erdman to his parents, written the night before his disappearance, had been withheld brought a sharp rebuke from District Attorney Earll. "Bring it tomorrow," he demanded.

There was a sharp contrast between the younger, more sophisticated, urbane, and well-dressed Albert Olson compared to the older, bearded, stoop-shouldered, shabbily dressed, and grieving Chris Olson. Yet in an inquest, appearances don't matter. What is being sought lies below the surface: the truth.

THE COURIER

$1.80 Per Year, in Advance — PRAIRIE DU CHIEN, CRAWFORD COUNTY, WIS., TUESDAY, DECEMBER 7, 1926

SKULL CRUSHED AND BURIED FAC

Erdman S. Olson Arch Criminal Sought by Police of Nation and 2 Foreign Countries

ther of the dead girl, Chris Olson, and her sister Alice and brother, Bernard and Andrew Helgerson were examined.

The parents of Erdman Olson, Mr. and Mrs. Albert Olson, their hired man, Edwin Knutson and Marie Anderson were also examined, together with James Nederloe, Chas. Bown, and coroner Otteson.

The testimony, in part, of Albert Olson and Chris Olson, is published

Letter Luring

Dear Friend:

I suppose you th haven't. I have been couple of operations.

I have decided th action. Now we'll not

(Top) *Chris Olson, father of slain 22-year-old Clara Olson, waits to testify during the December 6, 1926 inquest into her death.*
(Bottom) *Marie Anderson, Christie Anderson and Alice Olson, sister of slaying victim Clara Olson, attend the inquest into Olson's murder Dec. 6, 1926. Marie reportedly danced with Erdman Olson at Seneca the night Clara disappeared.*

CHAPTER 18

The Verdict

In the late afternoon District Attorney Earll started to wrap up the inquest. He wanted to complete it that same evening, but he was struggling to get all the witnesses' testimony. The local authorities wanted to be thorough and not appear to be rushed, lest criticism come back to haunt them later.

He called a variety of witnesses to establish points in rapid succession. First, he called two young women to the stand. They were cousins from Mt. Sterling, Marie and Christine Anderson. They were reported to have been Erdman Olson's partners at the Seneca dance on the night of September 9. Christine Anderson did not testify.

From them the authorities hoped to learn at what hour Erdman left the dance that night. District Attorney Earll questioned Marie Anderson as follows:

Q. How long have you known Erdman Olson?
A. I don't know, we went to school together almost all our lives.
Q. Was Erdman at the dance in Seneca on the night of September 9?
A. Yes.
Q. Did you dance with him?
A. I started to dance with him but I couldn't.

> Q. Why couldn't you?
> A. Because he could not keep step.

Here the district attorney did not ask if Erdman had been drinking, which might have been responsible for the fact that Erdman could not keep step with the music. She later related the drinking explanation to reporters.

> Q. What was your conversation with Erdman?
> A. He told me he was going back to school and asked me if I was teaching this year.
> Q. What time did you dance with Erdman?
> A. About midnight
> Q. Did you know when he left?
> A. No, I don't. I really paid no attention.

Marie Anderson's cousin, Christine Anderson, had also been subpoenaed to testify. There is no newspaper account or record of Christine Anderson being called to the witness stand. The inquest proceedings were taking longer than expected. The authorities were anxious to finish the same day. The funeral for Clara was scheduled the next day, on Tuesday, December 7. A howling snowstorm was battering Prairie du Chien. There was speculation that Christine Anderson would not substantially add to the narrative provided by Marie Anderson.

Bernard Olson, Clara's brother, was called to the stand. He testified as to his identity, and then District Attorney Earll zeroed in.

> Q. Do you recall the night that your sister left home?
> A. Yes.
> Q. Did you make observations of the tracks in the road the next day?
> A. Yes.
> Q. How were the tracks, were they all of the same kind or different?
> A. They were all the same kind of tire.

It should be noted, in passing, that this testimony conflicts with the earlier report that one tire was patched. On the morning of Clara's disappearance, Bernard, and his brother Adolph, inspected the tire tracks at the end of their driveway. One had been patched, and the tracks led north. Bernard reported his findings to his father. When Bernard visited the Albert Olson farmstead to confront Erdman, he did not find a patched tire. On the witness stand, Albert Olson testified that no tire on Erdman's Ford Roadster had been patched. Either Bernard was mistaken, or it was deemed not to be important.

Q. Did you go to Albert Olson's house after that?
A. Yes, I went over there to talk to the folks and to Erdman.
Q. Did you then have a talk with Erdman?
A. Yes.
Q. What was the conversation?
A. I asked Erdman if he was up late last night and after talking awhile I asked him if he came and took Clara away last night.
Q. What did he say?
A. He looked around a bit and then said he didn't.

Bernard then said he asked to see the car and to make comparisons with the tread and with the tracks he saw in the road. Erdman said it must have been some other car and invited him to the house to look for Clara.

Erdman's mother was anxious that I go through the house and the basement. I didn't want to, but she took me by the arm and coaxed me to look through the rooms. I finally did walk through the house. I told them I was not looking for Clara there, but that I want to know where she was.

Andrew Helgeson, a Mt. Sterling farmer, testified on the stand that he had gone to Galesville with Chris Olson on September 26. He said he had seen Erdman and heard Chris offer Erdman a place on the farm if he would come down and marry Clara.

Charles Bown testified he had found the spot where the body was buried, and James Nederloe, a member of the search party, said he had seen the body as it was taken from the grave.

Ernest Ottseson, undertaker, who removed the body, testified that he had charge of the body and was asked to identify clothing taken from her body in the examination.

Alice Olson, Clara's younger sister, was the next witness called in the inquest. She was dressed in black and wore a black veil

Q. Were you at home on September 9?
A. Yes.
Q. Did Clara get a letter that day?
A. Yes.
Q. Do you know who it was from?
A. Erdman Olson.
Q. Did she say it was from Erdman?
A. Yes. I asked Clara.

The district attorney then showed her an envelope and asked her to identify it.

Q. Is that the envelope the letter came in?
A. Yes. The address on the last letter had been printed.
Q. Did Clara go anywhere on September 9?
A. Yes, she went with Erdman at night.
Q. What time did Clara get the letter?
A. In the afternoon.
Q. What did she do after she got the letter?
A. She got out a geography book and looked at the map of the United States for a place she said she could not find.
A. What else did she do?
A. She burned all of her letters.
Q. Did you see her burn them?
A. Yes
Q. Did she leave any message?
A. Yes.

The district attorney displayed the clothes taken from her body, her comb, broken beads, and ring.

The Verdict

Q. Did these articles and the clothing belong to Clara?
A. Yes.

The police had carefully taken the mud-encrusted and waterlogged wad of letters and slowly dried the sheets, peeling them back one by one. A letter written in purple ink, written in the spring of 1926, was smeared and difficult to read. Erdman's name could be made out and a promise of marriage could be deciphered.

Yet the letter in pencil, the one Earll read aloud in the courtroom, was entirely legible and placed between sheets of glass to preserve their delicate nature. The letter proved that the murder was premeditated. When Earll showed it to Alice, the quiet dark-haired teenager looked at it with no emotion. "Yes, I seen it before; it's Erdman's handwriting.

"I was there when she got it. I saw her take it out of the envelope. I asked her who it was from, and she said Erdman."

The district attorney then took the stand and read the letter which Clara had received from Erdman. As the letter was read, there were gasps and whispers. Newspaper reporters scribbled furiously. A gavel silenced the crowd for a bit.

It was in Erdman's handwriting, and it laid the plan for their meeting the last night she was seen alive. It promised her they would go away and "get the ceremony over with, and then come back in a week or so."

The note urged her not to take any more clothing than she wore. It is evident, the jury was told, that the youth had in mind the disposition of the evidence, but despite this, the girl did take a few things, wrapped in paper. They were still missing. The letter from Erdman also instructed her to bring cash.

"Bring cash" was read twice. Testimony by the state pathologist and autopsy assistants had already established that Clara's purse was found in her hurried makeshift grave and that the purse was empty. A wave of whispered comments and conversation ripples through the courtroom. "The son-of-a-bitch not only clubbed her to death, he robbed her." "That low-down bastard." "Erdman is a dirty scum bag." And those were comments that could be printed.

Night comes early in December, and darkness had enveloped the Mississippi River town of Prairie du Chien when the last witness, District Attorney J. S. Earll, stepped down. According to reporters, the letter Mr. Earll read to the crowded courtroom was a stunning self-incrimination by Erdman. The six jury members thereupon removed themselves to a small annex room.

The verdict came ten minutes after fifteen witnesses had established a circumstantial case implicating the missing youth.

The official form was written down, and this is what the grand jury concluded:

The Verdict of the Jury, State of Wisconsin, County of Crawford

Before C.H. Speck, Justice of the Peace

An inquisition taken at the City of Prairie du Chien, in the County of Crawford on this 4th day of December 1926, before C. H. Speck one of the Justices of the Peace of the said County, upon the view of the body of Clara Dorothy Olson, there dead, by the jurors whose names are hereunto subscribed, who being duly sworn to inquire on behalf of the State of Wisconsin when, in what manner and by what means the said Clara Dorothy Olson came to her death, upon their oath do say:

We the jury find that Clara Dorothy Olson came to her death caused by a violent blow or blows administered by Erdman Olson, to the left side of her head, causing fracture of the skull and violent Hemorrhage probably in the early morning of September 10th, 1926.

In testimony whereof the said Justice of the Peace and the jurors of this inquest have hereunto set their hands the day and year aforesaid.

Signed: C. H. Speck, Justice of the Peace, followed by the signature of the six juror members. Henry Otto, J. H. Peacock, Roy Sheckler, Leo LaPointe, Edward McCloskey, Thomas E. Gander.

The charge of murder in the death of Clara Dorothy Olson was thereby declared upon youthful Erdman Olson, climaxing the sensational drama of illicit romance that had ended in the death of one and the disappearance of the other.

The December 4 edition of the *Prairie du Chien Courier-Press* newspaper gave an excellent summary of events leading up to the burial on December 2:

> Tragedy, born of a rural romance, has settled over the hills of western Wisconsin, where a shallow woodland grave yielded the body of Clara Olson
>
> From the gossip of farm girls, whose mothers remember the days when they spend the winter months at spinning, Crawford County has turned to discussion of the most dramatic episode in its history.
>
> Everywhere is the topic of romance of the 22-year-old daughter of Chris Olson and the 18-year-old Erdman Olson, son of a prosperous tobacco planter
>
> Clara Olson, whose farm home was near Seneca, met Erdman at a church social eighteen months ago.
>
> Erdman was a student at Gale College. It was easy see that Clara, the neighbor's daughter, living a life of rustic simplicity, should become interested in him. Her friends even were jealous.
>
> In eighteen months however, her romance ran its course. Erdman, charged with murder in a warrant sworn out by Chris Olson a week before a grim posse found Clara's body buried face down in a shallow grave near Rising Sun, on Battle Ridge, overlooking the home of Albert Olson, Erdman's father.
>
> It was Clara's first romance. She was one of nine children, satisfied with her lot. She had never been to a great city. There were occasional trips to historic Prairie du Chien, the county seat with its 3,000 inhabitants. Once she had visited La Crosse, Wisconsin, a city of 30,000.
>
> She "worked out" at a neighboring farm home because there were enough children at her father's house to do the chores. She willingly milked cows or did a man's work in the tobacco fields.
>
> The social life of the community, with the exception of the dances for Clara did not dance, satisfied her. She was a devout churchgoer.
>
> Not so with Erdman. He drove an automobile, wore good clothes, liked to dance, and enjoyed the company.

It made Clara happy to have Erdman, four years younger, call for her in his automobile, though he never entered her home. They took long rides through the picturesque Indian County during his school vacations. Clara was unaware, however, that Erdman boasted of his conquest of "that hick country girl" when he returned to school. She was ever a bit jealous, her sister revealed, that he attended dances with other girls, but she found solace in his numerous letters and the belief that he was her "regular beau."

Even before she disappeared, those stories of how Erdman boasted to his friends about his easy conquest of that hick girl began to drift back to Chris Olson in the summer of 1926. Clara also heard some rumors, and she must have harbored some doubts. The gossips had wondered if Clara was in for a heap of disappointment.

In the end, the most damning evidence was not contained in the testimony given by the fifteen witnesses. It is true that the youth's own father, Albert Olson, made grave admissions from the stand, in contrast to his earlier contentions. He admitted he knew of Clara's condition, because he had received a pitifully phrased letter from the girl August 17, begging that his son's name be given to her expected child. In fact, according to the testimony of Chris Olson, Erdman's father knew it before any other. Clara had written Erdman's father before she dared tell her own.

But the most striking testimony was given unwittingly by Clara herself. This was the note she placed against her heart when she crept out of her home at midnight to join Erdman in a secret marriage, so she thought, and which fell from her dress during the autopsy and was shown to the jury.

Early in the evening the inquest was over. It had been a long, exhausting day for all involved. Reporters rushed by people in an effort to be the first to file the verdict results. One man was knocked off his chair.

Of the immediate family, from which a dear one had been taken, only the father, Chris, sister Alice, and brother Bernard were in the courtroom when the verdict was read.

The parents of the accused slayer, Albert and Anna Olson, who had defended their son in testimony a few hours earlier, had already left.

The slain girl's father hesitated to leave the crowded courtroom even after the verdict. So much had been revealed about the fate of his daughter that he appeared to want to linger for a while. When all but a scattering of friends and neighbors who had crowded the room all day long had filed out, the father, holding feebly to the arm of his daughter Alice, walked slowly and with head bowed from the courtroom.

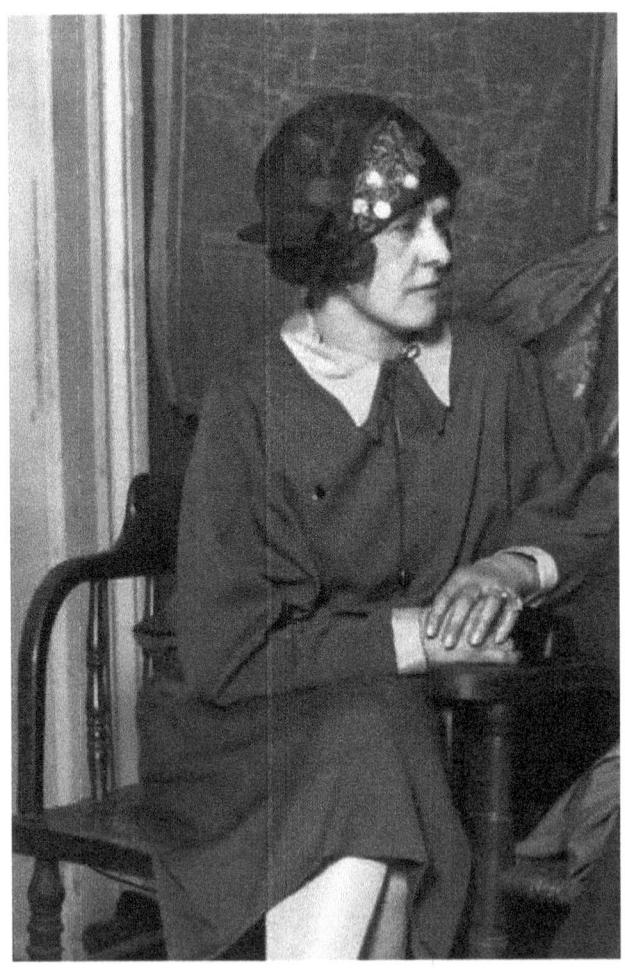

Marie Anderson testified on the witness stand on December 6, 1926. She was the last person to dance with Erdman Olson. She said he could not keep step.

CHAPTER 19

Laying Clara to Rest

The *Courier Press* in Prairie du Chien, on Tuesday December 7, gave an extensive account of finding the body and inquest transcript. In the style of the day, they used four headlines with ever decreasing type size and varying type style:

SKULL CRUSHED AND BURIED FACE DOWN

Erdman S. Olson Arch Criminal Sought by Police of Nation and 2 Foreign Countries.

DEATH-LURE LETTER FOUND INSIDE DRESS
ON SLAIN GIRL'S BODY

Jury Binds Heinous Crime and Damnable Insult
to Nation's Motherhood on Erdman Olson 18,
with Blue Blinkey Eyes and V Shaped Scar on Right Cheek.

One of the most mysterious murder cases of the decade was planned and perpetrated in the quiet confines of real Crawford county on the early morning of September 10, 1926. This by a rural youth given to violent temper when enraged, cast only reflection on the modern status of society.

Yet while the press was trumpeting headlines, a much quieter event had been taking place at Clara's home outside Seneca. After the autopsy, the slain young woman had been laid out in a gray coffin at the Otteson Funeral Home in Prairie du Chien. The casket was then transported to the Chris Olson family home on late Saturday night, December 4. That's because in the 1920s, a wake, the communal gathering before a funeral, was held in the homes of the deceased rather than at a funeral home. Friends and relatives would bring food, stay for some time expressing sorrow and condolences, and depart. This stems back to the custom in most Nordic countries in Europe for mourners to keep watch or vigil over their dead until they were buried.

Yet even this affair would not escape the notice of reporters. The December 6 edition of the *La Crosse Tribune* printed an article explaining why Chris Olson let his daughter go a few minutes after midnight on that horrible fall night. The headline ran: THOUGHT CLARA'S TRYST ELOPEMENT DECLARES FATHER.

Subheadline: DIDN'T INTERFERE BECAUSE HE WANTED TO SEE THEM MARRIED AND SETTLED DOWN.

The reason the press knew this came from a statement made by Mrs. Ed Isaacson, a cousin of the murdered girl. Mrs. Isaacson spent that Sunday with the Chris Olson family, taking flowers from La Crosse down to the farm home for the funeral.

According to her report, the casket lay in a darkened front room of the little white house. She saw Clara's mother rocking furiously back and forth. Beside a gray plush-covered casket, of which the lid hid the battered corpse of Clara Dorothy Olson, her brother Arthur, with tears coursing down his cheeks, swore an oath of vengeance against Erdman Olson. Above the casket hung a picture of Clara at age 13, attending her confirmation class at Utica Lutheran Church. There were few flowers to deck the coffin, while outside, a blizzard was blowing, the wind velocity increasing every hour, and the roads were piled with drifted snow. Flowers were not generally available in the dead of winter.

Arthur, the only one of the Olson children to have ventured any distance from home, was an electrical engineer in Milwaukee. The brother raised his fist and cried: "If I can get him, there won't be any trial. I'll fix him."

Emma, Clara's older sister by six years, came home from La Crosse. Emma was employed as a maid in a La Crosse hospital. Her parents had not told Emma that her sister was missing. They kept the story from her in the hope that she would return.

Mrs. Isaacson told reporters, "Mr. Olson told me that he thought when Clara left, that she was going to meet Erdman. But he only expected that they were going away to get married and that they were running away because of the trouble that had been made over their affair. He didn't want to interfere because he wanted to see them married and settle down, and he had been rather rough with Erdman just a little before that."

She continued, "It wasn't until weeks after Clara disappeared, and he had no word from her, that he began to worry and get suspicious. That's when he went up to Galesville and confronted Erdman. Even then he didn't push matters because he thought Erdman was taking care of Clara somewhere and everything would come out all right. But when Erdman disappeared and still no word came, he finally decided that everything wasn't right and started the investigation."

Chris would confirm this view himself when he later spoke to reporters. "Clara believed she was going to marry Erdman," he said. "She made three quilts this year and other things for her own home."

The funeral for Clara Olson was scheduled for Tuesday, December 7, and they did not want to postpone it. Hundreds of people had descended on Prairie du Chien, taxing the restaurants and hotels. The city was under blizzard conditions.

On Tuesday morning the dead daughter lay in her casket of gray in the farm home. Finding comfort in his ability to give his daughter a decent burial, Chris Olson gathered about him his wife, three sons and his five surviving daughters. A simple service at the home at eleven o'clock, led by Rev. Martin Finstad, afforded the family an opportunity for its last private leave-taking to their cherished one.

Ten miles away over the winding hills, the Utica Lutheran church was preparing for a public funeral with a sermon in English by Rev. Martin Dommeisnaes and another in Norwegian by Rev. Finstad. The church followed the design and style of many Lutheran churches in rural America. It was simple, stark, elegant, plain, and peaceful. After climbing six stone steps, entrance is gained through the thick wooden door. The church was only two miles from the home where Erdman Olson's parents lived and from the hill where the girl's body was found.

Finally, some floral pieces began finding their way to the home. The family would have a wreath of roses, the father said. The farmers and villagers of Seneca, Mt. Sterling, and Rising Sun would pay their respects to Clara Olson in a snowstorm. It was a sad and mournful day, with Christmas only two weeks away.

Rev. Finstad was met at the door of the Chris Olson farmhouse. He conducted simple private funeral services so that family members could say their last goodbyes. The casket was closed due to the condition of the body being buried for seven weeks.

A cortege of 150 automobiles drove slowly to the church, the largest funeral Crawford County had ever known. It started from the Olson home with the family and a few automobiles, but when the main road was reached, a little over a mile and a half away, an army of motorists was waiting in seemingly endless lines and fell in behind the mourners' cars.

The funeral procession accompanied the family and hearse the distance of seven miles to the Norwegian Lutheran Church, later to be called the Utica Lutheran Church. Many of the same people who attended the inquest in Prairie du Chien the day before came to her funeral. Services were scheduled for noon. It was the closing scene of the visitation of tragedy upon two families in the peaceful hills of Crawford County.

Six young men, Alfred Rand, Milard Musson, Clarence Aspenson, Orwin Olson, Telnar Olson, and Lawrence Uglen had been confirmed with Clara four years earlier. They now acted as pallbearers, carrying the casket from the hearse, up several steps, and set it on the carriage inside the entrance of the church. Wreaths bearing banners of "Sister" "Daughter" and "Clara" covered the casket.

An open grave had been dug several dozen yards north of the church, a mound of dirt in the cemetery on this hill marking the final resting place for Clara Olson.

Laying Clara to Rest

The church could seat only 150, but 300 crowded into the small edifice, packing all the pews, the center aisle, the two side aisles, the choir loft, and some had to stand. Another 300 stood outside amid the falling snow. Men shivered, stomped the ground, pounded their hands together, and shoved their hats and caps securely down over their ears. Yet they stood out in the open air, straining to hear the last words for Clara.

Chris Olson, old and haggard and crying, his wife, and their three sons and five remaining daughters sat in the front pews, all in black, the women wearing heavy veils close behind the gray plush coffin. They seemed to hear but few of the words that the Reverend Finstad had to say. The father looked up but once.

Rev Finstad opened with a prayer for the killer. "Let us pray for that boy who cruelly murdered this girl," he said. "Grant him repentance, O Lord, and forgive him through Thy blessings."

Rev. Finstad's text was based on the tenth verse of the 46th Psalm: "Be still and know that I am God." He blamed dancing, which he said leads to moonshine drinking and wild automobile rides, for the tragic fate of the girl. He adjured parents to keep their children from sinful dance halls. He mentioned particularly the one at Seneca where Erdman danced and drank the night Clara was killed, and others at Viroqua and Prairie du Chien.

"I would give a few words of warning to the boys and girls present here. Do not hide anything from your parents. If this rule had been followed by Clara and the boy who murdered her, such a crime would not have been committed.

"It is the duty of all parents to keep their children away from dance halls and to keep them from dancing. As a result of the exciting effects of modern dancing, various serious consequences are among the drinking of moonshine and wild automobile riding. Do not let your children ride around promiscuously in automobiles at all hours of the night.

"I confirmed Clara Olson. I always found her a pious, intelligent girl. She went out to meet her sweetheart. She had just bought a new dress, because she thought she was going on her wedding trip. It turned out to be a sad wedding trip, both for her and for him.

"Clara gave her life and her honor into the hands of this murderer and he deceived and betrayed her. But it is our duty to love and pray for the man who murdered Clara, just as Christ loved and when he was being crucified.

"The parents of the boy, I'm sure, are sorry for the parents of the girl, and I'm sorry for both," said the preacher. "Flaming youth, in its wild and headlong rush toward adventure and excitement, swept Clara Dorothy Olson to her tragic fate." She was a helpless victim of the rend of modern youth, in the words of the funeral orator.

The sermon by Rev. Finstad was followed by one in English delivered by Rev. Dommersnaes of Soldiers Grove. Soldiers Grove is but a few miles east, tucked in the bosom of the Kickapoo Valley. The name commemorates the soldiers who camped there in late July 1832 in their pursuit of Blackhawk and his Sauk tribe

When the service was over, the same six men who had been in Clara's confirmation class bore the coffin to the church entrance and then on to its short trip to the grave. The choir sang "We Shall Sleep, But Not Forever" in Norwegian as the grave was filled.

From the tiny churchyard, several hundred farm folks stood with bared heads while snow fell and the casket was lowered into the grave, then filled with shovels in the hands of eight young farmers. The outline of Battle Ridge could be seen across the ravines and gullies.

As the grave was being filled, the crowd slowly slipped away. The Olson girls—Minnie, Emma, Alice, Cornelia, and Inga—were crying and whimpering softly. The entire family stayed by the graveside until the soil had been heaped on the grave and patted down with shovels. The young woman had finally found a proper place to rest for all eternity.

News of the Day in Pictures | **THE MILWAUKEE SENTINEL** | *Pictorial Review of World Events*

Posse Combing Kickapoo Valley Hills Finds Grave of Missing Olson Girl

WOODS WHERE POSSE FOUND GIRLS BODY.

(Top left) *The Chris and Dina Olson family gather around Clara's casket several hours before the December 7, 1926 funeral. Seated: Mrs. Chris Olson and Albert Olson. Standing L to R: Bernard, Alice, Minnie, Arthur, Emma, Cornelia, Inga.*
(Top right) *Six young lads, all from Clara's confirmation class, carry Clara Olson from her home to a waiting hearse.*
(Bottom left) *The funeral procession for Clara Olson numbered over 150 cars.*
(Bottom right) *Graveside for Clara Olson. Clara was six months pregnant with a girl when she disappeared on September 26, 1926.*

CHAPTER 20

The News Spreads to the World

The farm people in the hill country of Rising Sun, Mt. Sterling, and Seneca did not get the news immediately about the inquest into the Clara Olson murder, resulting in the sensational finding that Erdman Olson committed murder. Few village and farm homes had radios. To get a newspaper, they had to travel, and for many, the only method of transportation from Prairie du Chien to the villages was a solitary bus that ran between Mount Sterling, Rising Sun, Seneca, and Gays Mills. There was just one paper, the weekly *Prairie du Chien Courier-Press*.

The most common way the news leaked out was through the Prairie du Chien telephone operator, who was also the town crier. News that trickled to her was telephoned to one citizen in each of the four smaller towns. They would hear the old-fashioned two long rings and three short rings on the phone. Each possessor of the phone would pick up the receiver and told the latest happenings. The little towns feverishly awaited the news, even a day late.

Still, in this case the news of the inquest was sent out every hour. How Clara Olson died and why Erdman Olson was guilty reached the telephone exchange in the northern villages far more quickly than normal.

For every story, however, there is a counterbalancing story. Even while the funeral for Clara was being held, Albert Olson went to Prairie du Chien to confer with friends on the advisability of hiring counsel in the interest of his son. "I won't believe that Erdman did it until I hear it from his own lips," the wealthy tobacco planter said defiantly.

Erdman's father had continued to express faith in the innocence of his son, No matter what the world might think, Albert held firm in his faith in his son. "Innocent? Why, I'll bet my last dollar on that kid of mine," he said, "and say I'll give a whole lot to send a message to my boy."

He then contacted radio stations, asking them to broadcast this message:

"Dear boy of mine. Come back, Erd boy. I'll stand by you until the last. I know you didn't have anything to do with the disappearance of Clara. Your mother is fine and knows you are innocent of any wrongdoing. It may look bad for you, boy, but trot along home to me, kid, never mind how black it may look. Try your damndest to get in touch with me. I'll do the rest."

Olson was reminded that it might cost him a great deal of money to prove the innocence of his boy. He was asked how many acres his farm contained.

"The hell with the acres. We'll start over again," he burst out. "Why, I have 280 acres of good land, valued at about $100 an acre, and buildings valued at close to $75,000, and I'll back it all on that kid of mine."

More than a few farmers in the nearby valleys and hills had a chuckle over Albert Olson's statement about the value of his land and buildings. Overheard at the Finley store was this remark: "Albert just might have exaggerated a bit on his place up there in Rising Sun." At the Mt. Sterling Lutheran Church after Sunday services, a man joked: "$100 an acre? He'd be lucky if he got $20 if he tried to sell."

Farther afield, newspapers went all out to sensationalize the Olson murder case. A few stretched the limits of credulity and some bordered on plain silliness. The *Chicago Herald*

Examiner hired Charles A. Bonniwell to do an evaluation of the personality of Erdman Olson. Bonniwell, billed as a famous "Character Analyst and Psychologist," performed this careful study by using a photograph of the young man.

The December 6, 1926, edition featured this headline:

> SECRETIVE EYES AND FEMININE
> FEATURES CHARACTERIZE OLSON
>
> DETERMINATION AND WEAKNESS
> SHOW HIS CONFLICTING NATURE

Erdman Olson impresses one at a casual glance as a secret personality—one who would do things and successfully hide the fact that he did them. That is set in his eyes, deep set and partially covered by the upper lids. The breadth of his forehead is indicative of excellent mentality. It shows ambition to progress, lift himself off the commonplace of farm life, eager to obtain an education, that would fit his for the role of a dilettante.

On the other hand, his forehead lacks depth, offsetting his mentality with a lack of moral stability. This quality is further evinced by his narrow-set eyes, indicating a particularly selfish nature.

The base of the nose is rather full and generally associated with those whose love is rarely on a spiritual plane. It is indicative also of histrionic talents and shows a tendency on Erdman Olson's part to pose. The mouth is rather full, distinctly feminine, and contour is indicative of weakness of character.

One of his pronounced features is the depth of chin, associated with strength of purpose and ability to hang on. The lobe of the ear is rather full and his combines with the size of the ear is that of a person who comes from long-lived stock. Its fullness tends partially to offset selfishness shown by eye and mouth.

The breadth of the face below the eyes is that of one whose instinct is to fight. This ordinarily strong quality, however is offset by the predominance of feminine characteristics, making him a receptive type.

We have in Erdman Olson a combination of aggressive receptive type, the male quality which is aggressive at times, offsetting the feminine, which is receptive. Consequently, a youth of this type would frequently get himself into trouble by being actuated by one set of qualities and unable to extricate himself because of the predominance of the receptive instinct.

Patriaci Dougherty of the *Chicago Herald Examiner* also interviewed Erdman's mother, Anna. "A new note was injected into Kickapoo Valley's tragedy by the woman who is most anxious to protect Erdman from the scorn of the world, his mother. She battled with her wits all yesterday morning on the witness stand to keep from giving damaging testimony against her firstborn."

Anna told the Chicago reporter, "Clara was four years older than Erdman. She wasn't as innocent as they try to make out. Erdman told his father that she had had sweethearts before, and I know that must be true, because Erdman was away at school at the time Clara must have got into trouble, if she was expecting her baby in December or January."

She continued, "Erdman didn't know how to resist the temptations Clara put in his way. His friends were all good girls that he met through school chums, and at dances. When he visited schoolmates during vacation, there was one girl in particular—a student at Gale College. She's a sweet little girl who belongs to a fine family, and she and Erdman were very fond of each other. He wrote her regularly, twice a week during vacation, and she wrote back in the very next mail.

"She was an innocent smart girl—the kind I'd want Erdman to marry when he was old enough. I guess when Erdman thought about what she'd think if he married Clara, he just couldn't do it."

For balance, the reporter also talked with Clara's younger sister and closest confidant, Alice. "Clara met Erdman at a basket social at Peter Severson's a year and a half ago," Alice told her. "She fell in love with him the minute she saw him, she told me afterward. I was at the party with a boy from Mount Sterling, and we four came home together. Erdman kept talking about Clara's pretty eyes. He was quite the smart fellow to hear talk, and I could tell from the way Clara looked at him that she was believing everything he said. He used to come over evenings in his car all that summer, and Clara used to go out with him. Sometimes they'd go driving, and sometimes they'd just pull up in a corner of the yard and sit there all evening. But Erdman never came in the house."

The newspaper writer hypothesized: "How was Clara, a little country 'hick' as her sweetheart called her, to know that Erdman's wooing was not the honorable method? She was the fifth of a family of girls and she had, for a precedent, only the drab lives of her older sisters, gradually fading into old maids, to guide her. She only knew that Erdman Olson, the college boy who drove his own car and wrote checks on his father's bank was romance, and she loved him for that fact alone."

"He went back to school in September 1925, and all winter Clara and he corresponded," Alice said. "And, when he came home for vacations he always came over to see her. She used to fuss with her clothes and make new things to wear when he came."

The *Chicago Herald Examiner* speculated:

> There is a new theory that Albert Olson knew of and consented to a clandestine wedding. The final letter Erdman wrote to Clara contained complete arrangements for a clandestine wedding, the lure that brought Clara from her home at midnight, and is the basis for a new belief expressed by authorities tonight that Albert Olson, wealthy father of the missing student, knew of and approved plans for the marriage.
>
> Abandoning the first theory, that the letter was merely a ruse, authorities now declare there is evidence to believe that young Olson actually had contemplated a secret marriage. They now believe Albert Olson offered financial support and all the help in his power to bring the scandal to that comparatively peaceful ending.
>
> And his silence on that aspect now, officials contend, is because he knew his son left home on the night of September 9 to take Clara away and marry her and that his admission of that salient fact would virtually convict his son of murder.
>
> Young Olson, stubborn, proud, convinced he was of a caste above the green country girl, consented to the wedding

as an expedient, according to the new theory, but confronted with the cold proceeding, flew into a frenzy and killed her.

Only a man wrought into a great frenzy could have struck the first blow that crushed the skull of the girl, making a great triangular fracture above her ear, the expert pathologist declared.

Several newspapers, including the *Winona Republican-Herald*, ran a story: "There is great excitement in the Kickapoo Valley and in Prairie du Chien when it was reported that Edwin Knutson, hired man on the farm on Albert Olson, was coming to the office of District Attorney J. S. Earll to talk."

Knutson did come when summoned and again declared that everything he knew had been told on the witness stand at the inquest, that there wasn't much use of "hounding him" each and every day because he couldn't tell any more than he had while under oath.

He said he was asleep in the Olson home at the hour the murder was committed. Now, was he ever a suitor of the slain girl? He had merely taken her home from a church social upon one occasion. Also, he knew nothing that might assist the authorities in their search for Olson or that might shed any light upon the slaying itself.

Parts of Knutson's previous story, viewed as filled with improbabilities or discrepancies, were the subject of considerable questioning as Earll continued to grill him. One of the most interesting of these was Knutson's statement that when he drove Erdman Olson to college at Galesville, a few days after Clara disappeared, not a word was uttered by either concerning her.

Some residents of Crawford County thought that Knutson knew more than he had stated, and on his return home the night of the questioning, he suffered a complete nervous breakdown. He was under the care of a physician when his father was sent for to come from Stanley, Wisconsin.

The young man's father subsequently related the conversation that followed the meeting. "They had told me about his collapse and that I shouldn't talk about the Olson case, so when I went in, I just said, 'Hello, Edwin, how are you feeling now?'

'A little better,'" he said. "I sat beside him for a bit and did not say much. We just gazed a bit. Then I said, 'Stick by the truth, my boy. It's always the best way.' He looked up at me and said, 'You wouldn't think that if you knew what I know.'

"I remembered what they told me and changed the subject, but when he gets stronger and better able to talk, I'm sure he'll tell me all that is on his mind. All I know about the case is what I've read in the papers," Mr. Knutson continued, "now I don't know what to think for from that statement of his; it seems certain that he's afraid of something."

Evar Nederloe, from Mt. Sterling, uncle of young Knutson, related that Knutson had eaten but little for days. Nederloe said that Edwin Knutson broke down under the long strain of questioning and while delirious, made those statements: "Murder! Murder! Murder! That's all I've heard! "She would stare at me and say she didn't have to be buried at night! "Hide in the cellar!" Regaining strength and mental coherency, by the next day, he explained he was unconsciously repeating remarks made to him by Mrs. Olson when investigators called at the farm.

"She told me to hide in the cellar," he said, "but I refused. I told her I had nothing to hide from. When Mrs. Olson said, 'She didn't have to be buried at night,' I think she meant it was not proved that Clara was buried the night of her disappearance. I was mighty nervous, particularly after the investigators were there, for they made Albert mighty angry—so mad he said to his wife, 'Get out my gun and some cartridges. I'm not going to be pestered anymore.'"

The *Winona Republican Herald* carried a story on December 15 about the shovel that Erdman may have used to dig the grave of Clara Olson:

> Tracing of the lost shovel believed to have been used in digging the grave in which Clara Olson was buried, was the latest development today in the Olson murder case. In the light of developments today, it is believed that the shovel was obtained from the grader of a highway patrol.

THEFT DATE IS CLUE: Andrew Munson, a road patrolman, reported to J. S. Earll, district attorney, that he had missed such a shovel about September 9, the date on which Clara was last seen alive by her family. "I didn't think much about it at the time, just figured it fell off the grader and was lost," said Munson.

"Lately I got to thinking about this murder, and it occurred to me the shovel used was probably mine." At the time of the slaying, Munson explained, "I was working on roads in the vicinity of the farm of Albert Olson," whose son, Erdman, Clara's sweetheart, now is being sought throughout the, country on a warrant charging him with the murder.

Used to dig grave when Clara's body was removed from the grave in which her murderer hurriedly had concealed it, experts declared positively the hollow had been dug with a round-nosed gravel shove. But nowhere could investigators ascertain where the slayer could have obtained the shovel.

Yet this possibility did not lead to anyone finding the shovel. Increasingly, as time passed after Clara Olson's funeral, the leads that authorities were searching for so desperately would enter the realm of speculation. Nowhere was this more true than the "sightings" of Erdman Olson that began to appear all over the country.

More Mystery in Clara Olson's Mysterious Murder

The Governor of Wisconsin, After a Year and a Half, Orders State Officials to Try to Find Out if the Girl's Runaway Sweetheart, a College Student, Crushed Her Skull and Buried Her in a Shallow Grave

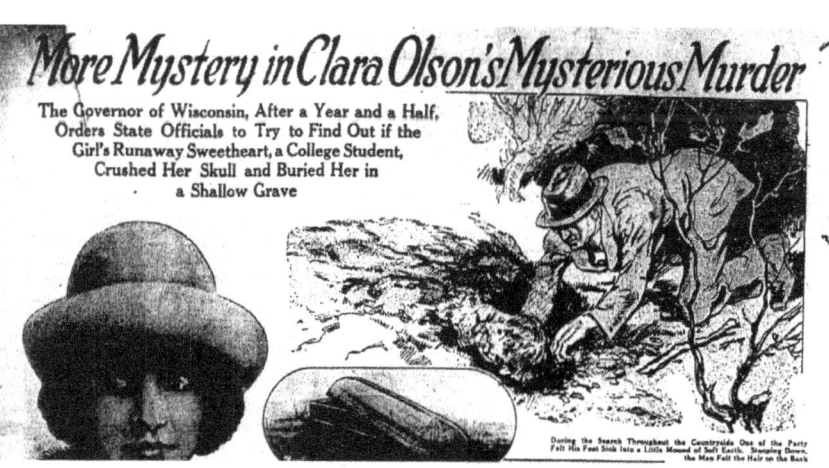

During the Search Throughout the Countryside One of the Party Felt His Foot Sink Into a Little Mound of Soft Earth. Stooping Down, the Man Felt the Hair on the Back

(Top) *On December 7, 1926, the body of Clara Olson was laid to rest in a grave a few yards from the Utica Lutheran Church. A snowstorm was in progress.*
(Bottom) *The murder of his daughter, Clara, aged Chris Olson beyond his 59 years.*

CHAPTER 21

The Search for a Killer

That Erdman Olson was supposedly sighted in so many locales around the land was simple. People wanted the reward money. A major contribution was made by Crawford County officials.

The county supervisors, many of them farmers, gravely went about their special meeting in the circuit court room in Prairie du Chien on December 10. Three days had passed since Clara Olson's funeral.

When Chairman James Fisher, banker-farmer from Eastman, suggested they add their "per diem" for attending a meeting to the reward, they arose as one man. This would add an estimated $200 to the total.

The board adopted this resolution after a speech by the district attorney. "This foul murder," he said, "is a blot on our county, and we must be as determined as possible, seeing that the man who committed it is brought to justice. It is a serious crime, and a substantial reward is necessary. I think it is a pity that the law will not allow the County Board to appropriate more than $1,000, and I therefore have already started a popular subscription."

It was expected a petition for additional reward would be sent to Governor Blaine for $500 with countywide contributions that would exceed $2,000 for anyone capturing or causing the arrest of the accused murderer. Chris Olson offered an additional reward of $200, a figure matched by the *Milwaukee Sentinel*. The newspaper printed a picture and description of Erdman Olson, including the clothes young Olson was wearing when he fled: a powder blue suit, a brown overcoat, light blue cap, oxblood shoes, size 8 or 8 1/2.

Arthur B. Curran, district attorney–elect, who would take office in January, commended the board for their alacrity and unanimity. "This murder," he said, "surpasses in brutality the Loeb-Leopold murder in Chicago. It is to be regretted that you cannot do more than you are doing."

The county board also appropriated $500 for the expense of the district attorney and sheriff to put circulars across the United States for the capture of Erdman Olson. Authorization of a tentative reward of $1,000 for his capture. Total rewards raised the figure to $5,000.

James Fisher, head of the board, issued a call for the meeting, which also would approve bills incurred by the district attorney and Sheriff Sherwood. He was convinced that the reward sum was sufficient to cause any officer to make this arrest single-handed. The general opinion of law enforcement in Prairie du Chien was that Erdman had slipped into Canada. "It will require 3 or 4 months for the Redcoats to get action. He will certainly be picked up, for $2,500 looks good to a Redcoat," the sheriff said.

Crawford County officials were roundly denounced by Arthur Olson of Milwaukee, brother of the slain girl, who charged they had been apathetic and lax throughout the entire handling of the case. "They haven't done a thing," complained Arthur. "No real search is being made for Erdman, but we will go to the ends of the world for him, if we have to."

On the opposite side, Erdman's well-to-do tobacco planter father pledged his last cent to vindicate his son. The boy's father added some little mystery to the case by his casual observation that the case already "has cost me considerable money."

The promise of reward money quickly led to a flood of sightings. The same *Winona Republican Herald* story on the missing shovel reported one of these:

Another clue in the now famous Olson murder case was run down here last night by Sheriff George Huck at the urgent request of Miss May Woods and several other Peterson residents who claimed that Erdman was to be found at a Minnesota City roadhouse. Sheriff Huck received several telephone calls from Miss Woods who insisted that a young man at a roadhouse owned by Mrs. William Shepard of Minneapolis was Erdman Olson.

Nothing was done about the matter until last night when a group of Peterson residents who called at the sheriff's office asked that the case be investigated. "I don't know Erdman, but I knew Clara Olson," Miss Woods who says her home is Prairie du Chien, told the officers. "And I know that there is a young fellow at the roadhouse who looks like Olson, says he is a college boy, and has played football and who is a nervous acting chap."

Miss Woods was so positive that the young man was Olson that she persuaded the sheriff to investigate. She displayed a telegram received from Sheriff Harry Sherwood of Crawford County, in which he asked the Winona sheriff to assist in running down the clue. The Winona sheriff, accompanied by another officer, and the Peterson residents drove to Minnesota City at 7 PM yesterday and got in touch with the youth who was believed to be Olson.

Indeed, the search for Erdman Olson would range from Norway to the state of Georgia. Police in Norway arrested a youth leaving a steamer from the United States. The Coast Guard had been alerted to watch for any young male fitting the description of Erdman Olson. Military recruiting offices were advised of the possibility that Erdman might try to enlist. Foreign ports were notified to be on the outlook for Erdman Olson, since Norway was the ancestral home of the Olson clan. The arrested youth in Norway was detained for a short time and released.

District Attorney Earll left on Thursday morning, December 9, for a secret trip to Mason City, Iowa, on some clue connected with the Olson case, the purpose of which was closely guarded. It was rumored that he was seeking additional information about Erdman Olson.

Al Sampey, chief of detectives in Springfield, Missouri, announced that for the last three days, officers had been combing Springfield in an effort to apprehend Erdman Olson. Chief Sampey said that a motorist who arrived here last Friday over the St. Louis highway reports having picked up a young man answering Olson's description and taking him as far as Marshfield. The youth said he was en route to Tulsa, Oklahoma.

While the nationwide publicity caused suspects answering the description of Olson to be held by police in eleven different cities, the mismatch in descriptions caused their release. For example, a body held at St. Louis was among them. It was another false identification.

Indianapolis police were searching for a youth identified as Olson. Four different people claimed to have met him looking for work, and there were numerous others. Nothing came of these sightings. "People will turn in their own mother for the promise of reward money," a grocer in Prairie du Chien was overheard to say.

Yet the most intriguing sighting involved the owner of a tobacco plantation, Charles McNeal. On November 13 he picked up a youth on the side of the road near Alma, Georgia. The youth gave his name as John Pittman. He was hired on the spot, and he roomed on the plantation with a youth by the name of A. J. Horman. The next Saturday, Horman "turned him in" to the sheriff on suspicion that he was Olson.

E. J. Thomann, a brick mason who was at work on a school building in the vicinity, said he became suspicious. The youth told conflicting stories about where he came from, including Baltimore, Miami, North Carolina, Chicago, and finally Wisconsin. He was unable to give any names or addresses of any person living in those places.

At a country dance Thomann and Pittman attended together, Pittman laughed at the way "they dance in the south" and described dances in Wisconsin. A few days later, the two were in town and at the approach of two policemen, Pittman said to Thomann, "Let's move on; they're watching me too closely."

At the time, Thomann was not aware that Erdman Olson was wanted for murder. He returned to Alma on November

20, and after reading newspaper accounts of the crime, saw a photograph of Olson published, which he said tallied with his recollection of Pittman, and he wired Sheriff Sherwood of Crawford County, Wisconsin.

Horman drove 300 miles to Columbus, Georgia, and telephoned Sheriff Young, of Charlestowne, in Kennesaw County, Georgia, that he could find a young fellow matching Erdman Olson's description. Horman told the sheriff that he should get the reward money.

An arrest quickly followed. Yet Pittman denied that he had any relatives. The youth was held at the Alma jailhouse. According to the description given by the sheriff, Pittman was five feet seven, weighed 150 pounds, parted his hair in the middle, and otherwise answered to the description of Olson. He had a scar under his right eye, which was mentioned in the official handbill. He gave his name as John Pittman and denied all knowledge of the letter he supposedly wrote to a lawyer, James B. Bowman, demanding a telegram by sent to Mervin Helgerson and asking for $1,000.

Bowman, in turn, was questioned. Bowman admitted to Alma mayor Thomas P. Stone that he had sent two telegrams to Mervin Helgerson, age 18, chum of Erdman Olson and son of a garage owner in Mt. Sterling, instructing him to come immediately. He later sent another message instructing Helgerson to send $1,000.

A decoy telegram was sent to the lawyer in an effort to check on the authenticity of his communication. A message was addressed to him at the Frances Marion hotel in Charleston. It said: "How much? Wire M. H. Signed 'A.' by M. H."

Young Helgerson consented to this wire being sent. It was calculated the lawyer, if his first telegram was authentic, would believe that M. H. stood for young Helgerson's initials and that the "A" would mean Erdman's father, Albert, was communicating with the lawyer for him through Helgerson.

Mayor Stone said he and police detectives talked with Bowman on Tuesday night and were told that he was meeting another man at ten o'clock. The mayor and detectives did not make themselves known, and when Bowman didn't meet his man, they drove him about the city in an automobile trying to find him. Then it was decided to hold Bowman again for further questioning.

Young Helgerson knew no reason, he said, why an attorney in Charleston would have communicated with him unless Erdman told him that Mervin had been an acquaintance of Erdman's.

Authorities could not see how the lawyer could have learned of the existence of young Helgerson unless Erdman told him of it. District Attorney Earll and Sheriff Sherwood declared that they believed Erdman must have appealed to the attorney and that the latter, not wishing to communicate directly with Erdman's father, had asked him for the name of some intimate friend he could trust. It was believed that Erdman must have studied the matter and decided that Helgerson was the one most trustworthy among his intimates.

Meanwhile, the Crawford County authorities were awaiting the arrival of a photo of a suspect. Photos of Pittman, however, proved that he was not Erdman Olson.

Meanwhile, "Bowman" was identified as an ex-pugilist whose real name was Jack Daley. He admitted that he was engaged to send the Helgerson telegram by one Patrick Deming, formerly known to the prize ring as "Kid Carter."

Finally, Crawford County authorities come to the conclusion that the Alma, Georgia, incident was a hoax. Unfortunately, it was only the first of several that would occur over the next few years.

The *Prairie du Chien Courier Press* quoted Sheriff Sherwood as saying, "Descriptions of Olson are being mailed and wired to all points requesting them. Many of the tips we receive daily appear to be likely and of course we are not passing any of them up, but there are so many that we are having difficulty following them all closely."

The Search Nearby

The dizzying number of sightings continued to mount, and by far the most came from places that had a more logical basis. These were from towns in the vicinity. Viroqua, not far to the north, produced a suspect. Sheriff Sherwood was routed from his bed at 2 AM. by calls that Olson was found in a hotel there. Yet as the inquiry developed, the sheriff said, he learned that a Milwaukee traveling man had caused the excitement, then disappeared.

In Milwaukee, numerous persons reported seeing Erdman Olson. F. O. Yost, superintendent of the Inland Steel Company mill, said a youth who obtained employment the previous Friday aroused his suspicions by his nervous and furtive actions. He failed to come to work on Saturday, but on Monday asked for his pay, saying he found the work too hard. It was remarked that he resembled photographs of Olson even to a scar on his cheek.

The Associated Press reported another sighting in Springfield, the state capital of Illinois:

> Police here wired Prairie du Chien, Wisconsin this afternoon that they had a man answering the description of Erdman Olson wanted for the murder of Clara Olson.
>
> The suspect has given his name as Norman Ludwig, aged 18, and his former home as Ashiphun, Wisconsin. He is held awaiting word from Prairie du Chien. Ludwig has been employed at the Monarch Tractor company plant here since the latter part of August or early September. He first claimed his age as 20 and told the officers that he knew nothing of the Olson murder or where it occurred.
>
> He later admitted he was 18 and that he had read of the case. Olson's double established his residence here last spring, his landlady told investigators. The convinced authorities are holding the suspect for positive proof. Ludwig, like so many others, was released after police determined he did not match the description of Erdman Olson.

From Poplar Bluff, Missouri, near the state line with Arkansas, came this report, filed in the December 9 edition of the *La Crosse Tribune*:

> Sheriff McCown and other officers today began search a for a young man answering the description of Erdman Olson, alleged slayer of Clara Olson, his sweetheart at Prairie, du Chien, Wisconsin.

J.L. Rawlston, superintendent of rural schools, reported to officers on his arrival here that the young man was given a ride in Rawlston's automobile last Wednesday night from the Arkansas state line to Poplar Bluff. He bore the complete description of Olson. The youth refused to discuss the Olson murder case and tried to conceal the fact that he was well educated. There was no arrest in this case.

Perhaps the wildest story, though, was reported by the *Winona Republican Herald* in their December 8 edition:

Ever since Erdman disappeared on September 27, police had been on the lookout, sending information to police units across the country. The pace has stepped up since the body of Clara Olson was discovered on December 2, checking with bus terminals, train stations, hotels, taxi companies. Authorities believe he is alive and on the run.

Three days after he dropped from sight at Gale College, Erdman Olson appeared in Winona, on October 1, police reported today, and announced he was going to the West Coast. John H. Firth of Winona told authorities he had given a "lift" west to a youth answering Erdman's description. He identified a photograph of the fugitive student. "I hope to see China before spring," he told me, said Firth.

Firth's wife and mother has positively identified the young man as Erdman Olson. On October 1, at 11 PM, Mr. and Mr. Firth and Mrs. Firth's mother were driving to St. Charles near Lewiston when they passed a boy who asked for a ride. He told then that he had run away from the National Guard camp at Sparta, and had slept in a barn near Dakota the previous night. "I am on my way to the western coast and expect to see China before spring. He declared at one time during the conversation that he gave his first name as Erdman. When asked again, the youth did not report his first name. He refused to give his last name. The boy was attired in a khaki shirt, a dark blue suit, cap and wore broad toed shoes He appeared to be about 18 years of age, weight about 165 pounds, and was 5 feet 7 inches tall. All the member of the automobile party took particular notice of a V shaped scar on the right side of the youth's face. He had a habit of blinking his eyes.

When a picture of Erdman Olson was printed in Monday's *Republican Herald Times*, all the members of the Firth family agreed that it was identical to the appearance of the youth they picked up on October 1. They thoroughly scrutinized the picture and could see no difference in any of the facial characteristics.

The boy said he had been given a ride from Dakota to Winona earlier in the morning. Mr. Firth said, "We picked him up near Lewiston and took him as far as St. Charles. Whenever a car passed, the youth seemed nervous, and when we left him off at St. Charles, he seemed frightened about something and kept looking behind whenever he heard a noise."

The youth told the Firths that he expected to get work on some passenger boat on the western coast and go to China for the winter. He expected to work his way, since he was short on funds.

Authorities from Crawford County are expected to come to Winona to interview Mr. Firth. All the ships bound for China have alerted to be on the lookout for the youth.

Not surprisingly, the sensational news that Erdman Olson has been spotted in Winona and was headed west flashed across the United States. But this spotting occurred in early October. By this point Erdman was believed to be long gone.

(Top) *Five sisters, three brothers, and parents Chris and Dina sob quietly as the casket is lowered in the Crawford County soil.*
(Bottom) *Clara Olson, along with siblings Minnie, Adolph, Bernard, Emma, Alice, and parents Chris and Dina are buried next to their home congregation of Utica Lutheran Church. A simple stone a few yards from Utica Lutheran Church, marks the end of a dream of marriage and family.*

CHAPTER 22

Grasping at Straws

As the mystery regarding Erdman Olson's escape grew, newspapers became rhapsodic. Comparisons to Theodore Dreiser's famous novel, *An American Tragedy*, and the Clara Olson murder case were being drawn by media outlets across America. Dreiser's 1925 narrative was made into a play that opened on New York's Broadway Longacre Theatre on October 11, 1926, even as Clara Olson lay face down in her makeshift tomb on Battle Ridge in northern Crawford County, Wisconsin.

Reporters for the *Winona Republican-Herald* turned to another literary inspiration when they interviewed people in Galesville and printed an account in their December 10 edition:

> A youthful Dr. Jekyll and Mr. Hyde. That is the Erdman Olson of conversation in Galesville, Wisconsin today. A smiling, clever, refined Dr. Jekyll, who had a winning way with the ladies, and who went "over big" with the boys who knew him well; yet considered a little high-headed by those young men who knew him only by sight.
>
> A cruel, torturing Mr. Hyde, who owned a gun and used it, who was bold, and never took a dare, and who was usually the source of any college prank or deviltry that might occur. This is the Erdman Olson that Galesville is talking about, and has been talking about for more than a week.

Yesterday, ten days after this little city broke into the crime limelight of the nation, merely through the fact that Olson went to school at Gale college, he and the Olson case served as the one subject of conversation. On the street groups of men dressed in heavy rough winter clothes, in the stores, in the homes, and everywhere, Erdman and the Olson case was the main topic.

"I try to not think of it," Rev. K. Lokensgard, president of the college, a fatherly man with a kind face revealed yesterday, as he sat in his little office, and did his best to be nice to another group of prying reporters. "Erdman was not much of a student. He did not apply himself to his studies. During the two weeks that he was here this fall he did not get started. He was back in his work from last year," he related. We know nothing of the crime. It is as much of a mystery to us as it is to the rest. I try not to think of it."

The formal statement issued by the school discloses that Erdman had been a disturbing element at Gale College. He was expelled last Easter, and the authorities were rather cold about taking him back. President Lokensgard's big heart opened to the bold carefree Erdman and took him in on probation. It is not hard to picture this fatherly man pleading with young Erdman to be good and abide by the rules. It is not hard to picture the "Dr. Jekyll Erdman" making sincere promises, or to picture the "Mr. Hyde Erdman" a few hours later planning a way to get even. And if half the tales one hears in Galesville were true, President Lokensgard must have the patience of Job or he would have taken this "black sheep" of the college by the neck and marched him off the grounds long ago.

"At the college we like to think as little about this case as possible and dismiss it as much as possible," President K. Lokensgard said yesterday. "Erdman was a disturbing element at the college and the only reason we took him back this fall was at the most urgent request of his parents. He was back in his work, seemed to loaf all the time, and was usually in some sort of trouble. Gale College has received much undesirable publicity from the Olson case, and for that reason I have nothing more to say about it. Were I in possession of any other facts, I would readily give them out."

The newspaper found a staunch supporter, though, in John Ottum, a clerk in a Galesville drug store and former Gale college student leader, said that he was well acquainted with Erdman. "I have known Erdman well for over a year," Ottum told the paper, "and I believe him innocent of all wrong. I saw him when he returned to school after September 14, and I had a long talk with him the morning he left on September 27. He always seemed quiet, calm, and cool. Nothing seemed to be on his mind, and I never suspected him of being in any trouble. How a man, who is supposed to have a guilty conscience like that, could act like he did, is more than I can figure out. When a fellow is down and out or has done something wrong, they will all know something bad about him or something which he has done in the past that has not been just right."

The newspaper added, "Ottum was one of few in Galesville who believe that Erdman is only a victim of circumstances. He is sincere in his belief, however, and says he will never believe Erdman slayed the girl until he hears Erdman, himself, admit it. He expressed some worry for his friend's safety."

Whatever the denizens of Gale felt about Olson was of no help to the Crawford County authorities. They wanted information that would help them locate the killer. District Attorney J. S. Earll and Sheriff Harry Sherwood had continued to question suspects and interview people with any knowledge of the murder. As part of that effort they went up in Galesville to interview classmates and roommates of Erdman Olson.

George Grinde, Erdman's roommate, said "that Erdman cried all night." That would be the night of Sunday, September 26, after Clara's father confronted him as to her whereabouts. Grinde, who slept in the bed next to Erdman's, declared, "Erdman tossed all night, and he just couldn't sleep."

Another friend, Tilman Mowe, drove Erdman to the bus depot on Monday morning. Mowe said Erdman was in tears and declared, "I have a feeling I'm going away on a long trip, but I'm really going just for a short time." Mowe told authorities Erdman wept openly but regained control of his emotions before the bus left. "He had two suitcases with him. He cried for quite awhile, and then he braced up."

Mowe drove Erdman to the Gardner hotel, and saw him take the bus to La Crosse, where he said he intended to undergo a minor operation on his nose.

Sheriff Harry Sherwood was reported in the newspapers as growing weary, working the case for up to 15 hours a day, getting little sleep, and discouraged by results of numerous suspects who had been arrested as the missing Erdman Olson, only to have them identified as someone else.

Murmurs had begun among the populace of Crawford County and surrounding environs about Wisconsin's death penalty. They were expressed in conversations and in letters to the editor. They followed along the lines of "they ought to hang that S.O.B. when they catch him."

Of course, Wisconsin does not have the death penalty. It was one of the earliest states to abolish capital punishment in 1853. Since Wisconsin was admitted to the Union in 1848, only one execution was performed, that one in 1851.

John McCaffary, an immigrant farmer from Ireland, was arrested and charged with the first-degree murder of his wife, Bridgett. It seems he drowned her in a backyard cistern at their home near Kenosha. After a two-week trial in May 1851, McCaffary was found guilty. The judge sentenced him to death by hanging, and the death warrant was signed by Governor Nelson Dewey.

McCaffary was strung up from a tree in front of the courthouse and jail in Kenosha with a crowd of 2,000 to 3,000 looking on. Some brought picnic lunches. The hanging did not go well, as McCaffary remained alive, struggling and kicking at the end of the rope for 20 minutes as he was slowly strangled.

The exhibition of McCaffary's slow demise in front of thousands of people prompted reformers to press for the abolition of the death penalty. Governor Leonard Farwell signed a law in July 1853 abolishing the death penalty and replacing it with life imprisonment.

The Ever-Dwindling Hunt

Sheriff Sherwood said that descriptions of Olson were being mailed and wired to all points requesting them, and indicated strongly that one of them would certainly produce the man being sought. Yet that was merely hope. The usual flood of reports that Olson had been seen or captured were rife but growing more tenuous, such as the theory the authorities worked on that he made his way into northwestern Canada and obtained employment as a lumberjack.

The newspapers soon began reporting sundry news that were not really discoveries. The Crawford county commissioner, for instance, decided to try to obtain a special fund to be posted as a reward for his capture and also appealed to Governor Blaine to offer a reward. Albert Olson wrote an open letter to urge his son to return and establish his innocence. His mother consulted a clairvoyant who assured her that her son was dead, presumably by suicide.

As so often happens in the news cycle, today's headline is yesterday's news. The Clara Olson murder case had the nation, indeed the world, enthralled for several days. But a mere week after she was committed to her permanent tomb beside the Lutheran Church on December 7, the story dropped off the front pages of most every newspaper.

Here and there stories appeared about sightings, arrests, and speculation on the whereabouts of her slayer, Erdman Olson. The *Winona Republican-Herald* printed a small story about the questioning on Edwin Knutson, hired hand on the Albert Olson farm, on one of the back pages.

The promise of a reward for any deed or discovery will bring out the fringe crowd, the weirdos, charlatans, and money-grubbers. Hence this headline in the December 15, 1926, issue of the *La Crosse Tribune*:

OLSON IN NORWAY MEDIUM "REVEALS";

EAU CLAIRE MAN TO START OUT IN SEARCH.

Dateline: "EAU Claire, Wis (A.P.) Because a medium in a trance "revealed" to him that Erdman Olson, 18-year-old Prairie du Chien youth, sought for slaying of his sweetheart, is now in Norway, B.C. Alf, 41, of Eau Claire, is planning the lad's capture.

He intends to work his way to Europe, locate the boy and claim the rewards for his arrest. Alf sought a picture of Olson today to aid in his search. He is firm in his belief that he will be successful.

A friend of his, he said, revealed the fugitive's whereabouts while in a trance. This friend, he declared, is gifted with spiritualistic power.

The boy was said by the medium to be residing in Norway with relatives but intends to go to another part of the country and establish himself in business. The medium also "revealed" that Erdman had spent some time in Eau Claire selling magazines while on his way to Winnipeg, which he left by ship to Norway from Quebec. Alf, who said he would start on the journey in a day or two, expects to divide his reward with his spiritualistic friend.

There was another story from Miami, Florida. A man thought by his fellow workers to be Erdman Olson disappeared an hour before police searched the home where he had been working. On information that a young man resembling Olson had been working at odd jobs for a week on lower South Bayshore Drive, officers hurried to the place to learn the suspect had "gone to lunch" at 10:30 AM. A cordon of plainclothes men were stationed around the house, but he did not return. Workers at the house said he was Swedish in appearance, and they identified a newspaper picture of Olson as the suspect.

The surest sign that reporters were reaching their wits' end trying to dream up a new angle was the turn toward the supernatural. One story that garnered headlines, on December 16, ran under a *La Crosse Tribune* headline:

NEWSPAPER MAN ADVANCES THEORY THAT

CLARA OLSON WAS ALIVE AFTER SEPT. 9

A theory that Clara Olson, Crawford County girl for the murder whom Erdman Olson, her sweetheart, is being sought in all corners of the compass, was alive nine days after the night of September 9, when her death is presumed to been caused by the Gale college youth, has been advanced by a newspaperman on the staff of the *Star-Courier*, at Kewanee, Illinois.

Paul R. Nesgen, through the office of the Star-Courier has informed District Attorney J. S. Earll, at Prairie du Chien, of giving a girl who answers the description of Clara Olson, a ride from Stoughton to Dixon, Ill. When he was returning from his vacation last September 18. Mr. Nesgen says the girl he gave a lift on the country road resembles the picture of Clara broadcast in newspapers throughout the country.

Nesgen says he encountered the girl a short distance out of Stoughton on September 18 and stopped to give her a lift when she waved to him. Without divulging her identify, the girl informed Nesgen that she was bound for Chicago. She maintained that she and three other girls were on a hike from Chicago to the Twin Cities and that she had left the others and was on her way back to Chicago.

The conversation led to the girl's occupation, Nesgen says, when the girl claimed that she was a Y.W.C.A. worker and could produce a card of identification. She talked on various subjects but appeared not inclined to speak of anything by which she might be positively identified. The girl was inexperienced and for some reason refrained from telling the exact truth. She wore an orange-colored dress, silk hose, and high-heeled slippers and carried a gray spring coat and shopping bag.

Nesgen said he advised, upon leaving her at Dixon, to go to the Y.W.C.A. or city matron for help when she arrived in Chicago and advised her to be careful of the people with whom she traveled if she decided to leave that night for Chicago.

Perhaps that bizarre story inspired the one that appeared on December 19, 1926: two weeks after Clara's dearth, Frank Blazek of Prairie Du Chien reported seeing her ghost "flitting over the snow, crying for her sweetheart."

In a more practical realm, at the Crawford County seat of Prairie du Chien, the officials elected in November were sworn in on January 3, 1927, for a term of two years. Arthur B.

Curran was the new district attorney, and Ernest S. Otteson the new coroner.

Among the changing of the guard, Emmet L. Haggerty became the new sheriff. Sheriff Haggerty was questioned about the apprehension of his most famous criminal at large:

> I believe in using common sense and lots of hard work and surely believe that the apprehension of Erdman Olson will be made within six months. The law will outwit the criminal and while the murderer's first instinct is to flee and hide, the human conscience is a powerful force, and sooner or later an attempt will be made by him to communicate with friends or relatives. Erdman will get awfully lonesome from constantly dodging people, and his own knowledge of his guilt will bring him back to Crawford County."
>
> Methodical work will often succeed where scientific deduction fails and with the countrywide distribution of these 10,000 circulars and every officer anxious to get that $2,500, it looks as though the young man will have a very difficult time to dodge the law for longer than two or three months.

Two months after the discovery of Clara Olson's body on Battle Ridge came this headline:

YOUTH FOUND DEAD NEAR OLSON GRAVE

JAMES HOLMES SUICIDE SHOT IN HEART BY HOLLOW TREE

The body of Will Holmes, 19 years, old, was found today by his father, James Holmes of Gays Mills, in a hollow tree in the Kickapoo River bottoms not far from the shallow grave where Clara Olson, sweetheart of Erdman Olson, was buried. A wound in his heart and a pistol, found at the base of the tree, were mute evidence of the tragedy. Relatives said Holmes had brooded over the fact that a Prairie du Chien high school girl had broken off her friendship with him.

Holmes had been to Prairie recently to visit his sweetheart Lydia Drake, who, it was rumored, had broken relations with him following a lover's quarrel. He had received a letter last Tuesday it is reported, which perturbed him considerably.

More time than that would pass before another sobering discovery was made nearby. At last the missing element of Clara's flight on that fateful night was found. The March 29, 1927, *Prairie du Chien Courier Press* covered that story:

CLARA OLSON'S WEDDING DRESSES
HID NEAR CRUDE GRAVE FOUND SUNDAY

SEARCHING PARTIES TO CONTINUE
UNTIL INSTRUMENT USED IN CAUSING DEATH BLOW
TO EXPECTANT MOTHER ARE PRODUCED
AS ADDITIONAL EVIDENCE

Chris Olson of Seneca, accompanied by daughter, Alice, and son Bernard, where here with L.S. Tichenor of Mt. Sterling Monday afternoon (March 28, 1927) to identify the bundle of clothing found on Battle Ridge Sunday afternoon by Raymond Henderson and his father, Bert.

Sheriff Haggerty, before showing the clothes to Alice, had her describe them, which she did perfectly. Both the brokenhearted father and sorrowing sister and brother readily identified the clothing as that which Clara had taken from home September 9, 1926.

The search was started Sunday morning by a group of eleven men, including Chris Olson, and they had hoped to find the instrument which was used by the murderer to kill Clara, and also the missing hat and bundle of clothing that Clara had taken with her the eventful night.

The first party of searchers discovered no new traces except a few yards north of the shallow grave a few shovels of dirt had been dug from under a small cliff. The digger had found the soil here only a few inches deep and too shallow for the burial of the body.

In the afternoon, Mr. Henderson and his son Raymond, who live close to Albert's, heard of the fruitless search of the morning, started out alone. After an hour and a half, they discovered the missing clothing about twenty-four feet from the Black River Road and equal distance from the land that turns down to Albert's. The clothing was inside a pasteboard box tied with two corset strings, and the new tan felt hat was tied to the outside. The box was sitting on end in a narrow cleft between two tree stumps and a small sapling. While it was in open view, the nature of the undergrowth in that particular stretch of cut-over woodland prevented its being seen other than by a keen-eyed woodman.

Authorities noted the fact that the bundle was but a short distance, about two city blocks, from the grave, and between that spot and Erdman's home.

The sadly dilapidated box contained two dresses, one a yellow polka dot and the other a tan dress that undoubtedly would have been Clara's wedding gown, a white silk slipper, two pairs of silk stockings, grey and tan, a number of safety pins, a packet of needles, and a small service pin, of the type popular during the war, with a single star. It was labeled in the press as Clara's wedding trousseau.

This discovery answered a final mystery of what had happened to the farmer's daughter. She had thought her newly bought clothes represented a grand step toward a new life. Yet they ended up being only an extra annoyance that a killer had to hide before his work that night was done.

Clara Olson

The photo of Walter Christensen (center) is typical of the grainy pictures printed in 1926 newspapers. L-R: Crawford County Sheriff Harry Sherwood, Christensen, and Chief of Police Stack of Dwight, Illinois.

CHAPTER 23

Erdman's Parents Demand a Review

Life went on in the hill country of Crawford County in southwestern Wisconsin. The dead were buried, and the living had to go on living and making a living. The murder of Clara Olson and the disappearance of Erdman Olson would come up often in conversations at church picnics, quilting parties, the threshing ring, butchering time, and wherever and whenever Norwegian families gathered. Norwegian Lutheran pastors would allude to the fall and winter happenings of 1926 as a warning to the youth in their congregations.

The snows in the hills and valleys melted, water rushing down the many creeks to the Kickapoo, Wisconsin, and Mississippi Rivers. The fields greened, the foliage returned to the trees, and lambs, piglets, calves, and foals were born.

The tobacco beds were prepared. Tiny seeds were planted in small pots in early May, covered with fine tobacco cloth, and watered. When four inches tall, the seedlings were planted in the fields around June 1. The oats and wheat seeds were in the ground, and the corn planting was close behind. Farmers would keep a close watch on the growth of the clover fields. Haying time was near.

A startling development in the Clara Olson murder case unfolded in the early summer of 1928. The headline in the June 5 issue of the *Prairie du Chien Courier Press* read: QUIZ ON OLSON CASE STARTED HERE TODAY.

Albert and Anna Olson had gone to Madison to see Governor Fred R. Zimmerman. They complained to Governor Zimmerman that the stain of the crime still remained on their son's name. Their son was still missing, and the circumstances about the time of the crime and afterward were worth investigation. The governor agreed some action would be taken.

His decision was also spurred by word from Chicago that Martin Gilbert, 48, of Detroit, was being held there after declaring he knew the girl's slayer. What's more, the man claimed to have killed Erdman Olson. The governor authorized Hugh Minahan, deputy attorney general, to begin extradition proceedings at once to bring Gilbert to Wisconsin.

At the same time the Governor sent J. E. Messerschmidt of the Attorney General's Office to Prairie du Chien to begin the investigation of the Olson case. He said he expected to spend several days investigating all angles of the case and would talk not only to Albert and Chris Olson but also to the many witnesses who had been called upon at the inquest.

His first step was to examine the letter found on Clara, along with those both she and Erdman had written. He also examined the moldy and clay-encrusted garments that Clara wore the fateful night she had gone to her death. The trousseau that was found six months later also was scrutinized.

The residents of Crawford County could not understand this move. Albert Olson explained that he wanted to clear the boy's name, but his neighbors asked why, if the college boy was innocent, he didn't come out of hiding and explain away the evidence against him.

Erdman's parents had devised a new theory. They did not believe their son was the killer but claimed that the youth himself was murdered at about the same time that his sweetheart met them. They also claimed in their talk to the governor that they believed Erdman's body would be found in the same Kickapoo valley. The county's probe was not thorough enough. Oddly, they particularly wanted to inquire into the alleged dream of Chris Olson's.

What argument did the Albert Olson family have? They claimed that just because Erdman had made an appointment to agree reluctantly to marriage and that on the way to that meeting, the side of Clara's head was smashed in with a club, did not prove that he was guilty. Women alone in the country at night had been murdered by strangers passing through.

That's all well and good, said the folks in the Crawford County countryside. But if he had nothing to do the crime, why didn't he come forward and explain what happened? If he failed to keep the rendezvous with his lover, he must have been somewhere else, and as he could hardly have been doing anything worse, there was every motive for him to produce his alibi. There are stories of men so honorable that they preferred the danger of being hanged rather than compromise some girl with whom they had been out, but Erdman's treatment of Clara revealed no signs of any such chivalry.

On the other hand, if he did keep the tryst and failed to find the girl, why didn't he write or call for an explanation?

If he arrived on the scene in time to witness the murder by someone else, why didn't he sound an alarm at the time and tell what he saw afterward? Or, if he came across her dead body, why did he say nothing and, in that case, who buried her?

The whole country knew about his vow that he would never be taken alive. If innocent, why should he fear being taken alive, people asked. Why did he write that letter asking her to sneak out?

As for Chris Olson's dream that his daughter was lying face down in a grave, that is not a prediction. Only after Clara's body was discovered in the shallow grave and he was told she was buried face down did he continually tell his neighbors and reporters about his dream.

At the inquest, Albert Olson had taken an indignant attitude. His son had run away because he was being coerced into an undesired marriage because of a condition for which he was not responsible. Now he was hinting that another man in the vicinity was to blame for her getting pregnant and therefore presumably for the murder itself.

When asked by reporters, Chris laughed for the first time since his daughter disappeared when he was told that Erdman's farther had asked Governor Zimmermann to see that the boy got justice.

"That's exactly what I want," said Chris, "and if he really wants it, all he has to do is make the young man come back here and tell us a few things. One of his family could claim the reward that is on his head, and it would be enough to pay his expenses from Argentina or where ever he is hid and nicely profit. Nobody can make him marry my poor girl now, and nobody is going hurt him. But he has got to answer some questions or stand trial."

Chris was reminded that Erdman's father had given to the press an open letter, urging the boy to return at once and establish his innocence. At that Chris laughed a second time, and he laughed once more when he was told that the fugitive's mother had consulted a clairvoyant who had assured her that Erdman was dead, presumably by suicide.

"Let the clairvoyant tell us where his body is, and if we find it, I'll believe him," Chris responded. "As long as that indictment stands, if Erdman is identified most anywhere in the civilized world, he will be brought back and get justice whether he wants it or not. But if the governor's John Doe proceedings cause the indictment to be quashed, and he is seen, he can hide again. I don't see any justice in that."

The people of Crawford County generally agreed with Chris, and they did not believe that the proceedings the Attorney General's Office had started would end with whitewashing a fugitive from justice in the absence of any evidence that he was dead.

After several weeks, Assistant Attorney General J. E. Messerschmidt reported back to the governor that there was no doubt of Erdman Olson's guilt.

He stated that there was sufficient evidence to try him for first-degree murder "when and if he is found":

> From my investigation, I have been forced to the conclusion that there can be no doubt but that Erdman Olson killed

Clara Olson. It is not necessary to hold a John Doe proceeding as a warrant has already been issued, and if that warrant were dismissed, a new warrant could easily be issued, for any number of persons could be found who would be willing to swear to a complaint charging Erdman Olson with murder the first degree. I would not hesitate myself to make such a complaint.

It appears that Erdman Olson left for parts unknown before it was generally believed that he had murdered Clara Olson. His parents told me that they know that he was not guilty. They based this belief, however, upon the statement that he was at home and it was impossible for him to have committed the offense. Some have argued that he did not have time to dig the grave and bury Clara Olson on the night of September 9 and arrive at home at 1:15 AM. I have carefully examined into this phase of the case.

This crime could have been committed by Erdman Olson without an accomplice. The grave in which Clara Olson was buried is in his uncle's woods out of view from the road in what might be called a lover's lane. He may have frequented this place with Clara Olson before, and it would have been an easy matter for him to have induced her to go with him to that place. Indications are that he dragged her to the grave by her feet.

With this reexamination of the evidence vanished the last hopes of his parents that Erdman would be exonerated. Yet the hope for justice in the case was also evaporating. Whatever end Erdman had or would come to, he would not spend the rest of his life in a prison cell for the crime of murder.

(Top) *Clara Olson's simple marker in Utica Lutheran Cemetery.*
(Bottom) *Chris and Dina Olson, parents of 10 children, went to their grave knowing what happened to their daughter but never able to see her killer brought to justice.*

CHAPTER 24
The Trail Goes Cold

In the weeks, months, and years following the disappearance of Erdman Olson, dozens of young men were arrested, taken in for identification, questioned, and then released. While the results were invariably disappointing, news editors never tired of featuring a possible resolution of the romantic case. Typical was the headline for January 18, 1932 some five years after the murder: ANOTHER 'ERDMAN OLSON' IS FOUND.

> Although very skeptical of the meager identification, Los Angeles police were holding a young man on suspicion that he may be Erdman Olson, who has been hunted since 1926, when the body of his sweetheart, Clara Olson, was found buried in a patch of woods in Crawford county, Wisconsin.
>
> The man was picked up after a transient, Edward Hess, showed a reward circular to two policemen on the street and point him out in a group of street corner loungers. The suspect laughed at the identification, saying that he was Jerome Hageman, 23.
>
> Hageman bears some resemblance to the description and the poor picture of Olson given on the reward circular, but police said that he probably would be released after Wisconsin authorities had looked over a photograph and fingerprint, for his man has brown eyes, whereas Olson's were blue.

On June 18, 1933, the *Milwaukee Sentinel* posted this front-page headline: TONSILS AGAIN SAVE THIS ERDMAN OLSON. A man calling himself Al Hartman was arrested in Portage, Wisconsin. The article went on to say, "Al Hartman still had his tonsils today and as a consequence, still had his liberty. Hartman looks like Erdman Olson, and he was picked up by county authorities who were looking for the Prairie Du Chien killer. After a night in the county jail, a physician was called and peered down Hartman's throat. The doctor shook his head. Olson's tonsils had been removed, and Hartman's were still in place."

The December 18 edition of *The La Crosse Tribune* ran a sighting under the headline: OLSON HAD NO SCAR ON FACE, SAYS CRAWFORD CO. SHERIFF. After running down so many leads, Sheriff Sherwood had finally had enough. He would issue a more complete description of Erdman Olson to narrow down the claims. The article read, in part:

> The youth held gave his name as Morris Mandell and claimed to live in North Dakota, although not giving the name of the city. He had been working at the Mr. L. F. Easton farm near the city and was released a few minutes after Sherwood's arrival and was taken back to the farm by Officer Bradley.
>
> Mandell, however, bore a striking resemblance to the first picture of Erdman Olson issued. He had auburn hair and had a scar under his left eye. He was a "dead ringer" for the picture, to quote local officials of the sheriff's department.
>
> However, one of the important features arising out of Sherwood's visit concerned with the scar which Olson is supposed to carry. Undersheriff Walter J. Rice, puzzled over conflicting reports concerning the scar on Olson face, asked Sherwood under which eye the scare was supposed to be.
>
> "He has no scar," said the sheriff.
>
> A more complete description of Erdman Sanford Olson is now being issued by Sherwood, which includes a picture which is supposed to be the best obtained of Olson. It is an enlargement from a Kodak snapshot, and although of necessity retouched, gives a much better conception of Olson's appearance.

Iowa City, Iowa, police were the next to hold a youth on the suspicion that he was Erdman Olson, reported the December 21, 1926, edition of the *La Crosse Tribune.*

The young man gives the name of Willard Matthew and refused to talk. His description tallies with that of Olson. He is described by police as five feet six inches tall weight about 125 pounds, a scar on his left cheek just under an eye, and is about 22 years old. Fingerprints and photograph are being sent to Wisconsin today.

The youth aroused suspicions of a farmer when bummed a ride but indicated to avoid the town as the farmer's automobile approached the city limits. He was arrested soon after in the railroad yards and held on a technical charge. Willard Matthew was released when he did not fit the description of Erdman Olson.

The occult element, always eager to help with unsolved cold cases, would make a reappearance, this time with a new twist. The following article emblazoned the front page of the December 20, 1926, edition of the *La Crosse Tribune*:

MEDIUM SAYS ERDMAN OLSON IS MURDERED

A.F. Roberts, Milwaukee, Widely Known Medium, Says Clara's Slayer Was Killed by Two Men.

CERTAIN BODY WILL BE FOUND IN SHALLOW GRAVE NEAR HOME.

Seer offers to Post Wager of $4,000 that Erdman's Body Will be Found

Milwaukee, Wi—That Erdman Olson, accused slayer of his sweetheart, Clara Olson, has himself been murdered and lies buried in a shallow grave at the edge of a swamp ten miles from his home, is the latest addition to a long list of weird features attaching to Wisconsin's outstanding murder mystery which began with the disappearance of the country girl on the night of September 9.

A. F. Roberts, widely known medium and seer, whose past record is said to be a succession of triumphs in clearing up mysteries in and about Milwaukee, is responsible for the statement that Erdman is not alive and that his body will be found as he has indicated.

So certain is the seer of his convictions that he has offered to post a certified check for $4,000 that young Erdman will be found dead.

"Erdman was killed by two men four weeks after Clara disappeared," Mr. Roberts said. "They laid him down in a grave at the edge of a swamp ten miles from his home. A forked tree stands near his grave."

Authorities in Peoria, Illinois, who were holding a youth from Fennimore, Wisconsin, Robert Harrington, who resembled pictures of Erdman, released him when an insurance salesman acquaintance with Harrington's family identified him. A moonshine "gag" was responsible for Harrington's making a wild statement that caused his arrest.

"Clues are petering out," Sheriff Sherwood told the Associated Press after the incident. He attributed this to the fact that authorities around the country now had an accurate description of the fugitive. "An inaccurate description of Olson was sent out by private detectives, and this caused us much annoyance through being flooded with reports that he had been found," Sheriff Sherwood said.

Still, numerous places had Erdman Olson holed up at one time or another. He was spotted in Indianapolis, a monastery in La Crosse, Wisconsin, hitchhiking in Kansas, living by the rail yards in Minnesota, and even hiding in a secret room in the Albert Olson house.

The number of leads diminished over the years and then decades. Clara Olson's killer had pulled off that rare feat in the annals of justice. He had managed to evade capture and imprisonment for a capital crime. As late as 1949, however, another "bounty hunter" seeking the reward money would point a finger at someone purported to be, 23 long years later, Erdman Olson.

The *Winona Republican-Herald* carried a story in their December 16 edition. Ted Wagner, a packing plant worker, was arrested in Fargo, North Dakota, as Erdman Olson. The warrant for Wagner's arrest was signed in Fargo by J. Edward Dolan. Dolan had told authorities he was "positive" about the identification since he "grew up" with Olson in Wisconsin. Dolan attested in letters to the Crawford county judge he was certain Wagner was the wanted man.

Dolan told police he had been working the Armour packing plant only few days when he recognized Wagner, a fellow employee. Dolan said he had even engaged a room at the Fargo rooming house where Wagner have been employed at the time, so he could keep an eye on him. When questioned by a reporter, a plant foreman at Armour said Dolan considered himself a detective story writer and somewhat of an amateur sleuth.

> Wagner gave his age as 46. At the time of the murder warrant was issued, Erdman Olson was 18. Today, 23 years later, Olson's age would be 41. Wagner, father of four daughters, has denied any connection in the slaying. He is employed at the West Fargo Armour Packing Company plant. His wife died at Jamestown, N.D. in 1947. When Wagner was taken into custody, care of two of his children was turned over to the county detention home at Fargo pending his return.
>
> Wagner also manages a rooming house at Fargo. His wife died March 11, 1947. Their daughters are 15, 12, 10 and 4 years old. Wagner said he was shocked at his arrest. "I don't know why I was arrested," he said. "It came as a shock to me. I am a German, and Olson supposed to be Norwegian. I've never gone by the name Olson. He is supposed to have had a college education, and I never went beyond the second grade. This is the first time I have even been in Wisconsin."
>
> Wagner's arrest followed the receipt of a letter at Prairie du Chien from Dolan who said he worked with Wagner at Fargo and had known Erdman Olson when they were boys at Rising Sun, Wisconsin.
>
> "I feel sorry for that fellow [Wagner], said Bernard Olson, as he stepped off the train which brought Wagner here. "I knew Erdman Olson well enough to spot him from the back.

I wouldn't even need to see his face. This certainly is not Erdman Olson."

Harry Sherwood, sheriff at the time of the slaying, echoed the statement. Sherwood and Earl Stunkard, undersheriff at the time, had accompanied Day and Bernard Olson to Fargo. Wagner was taken to Prairie du Chien, accompanied by the four men.

Wagner was taken to the county jail, where he was booked on a charge of suspicion of murder. Day said that relatives of both Erdman and Clara Olson would be asked to attempt identification later today. Asked whether Wagner was Erdman Olson, Sherwood answered, "No, I am certain it is not Erdman." Stunkard, when asked the same question, said, "I won't commit myself."

In his letter to Crawford County authorities, accuser Dolan also wrote, "I am writing to the *Chicago Daily Tribune* for the sale of 'scoop' on the story also to *True Detective* magazine as I believe they also offered a reward for the capture after the crime was committed."

Therein lies the true motivation behind the identification. J. Edward Dolan was exposed as yet another in a long line of opportunists who were encouraged by the smell of reward money. Theodore Wagner of Fargo, North Dakota, was not the last person arrested or detained on suspicion of being Erdman Olson, but for all intents and purposes, the path he had taken to escape would remain forever unknown.

Epilogue

People in the hills and valleys of the Kickapoo River and Crawford County still talk about the Clara Olson murder some 90 years later. The elderly folks remember hearing stories from their parents, aunts and uncles, and retired neighbors. "My dad helped in the search" or "My folks attended the funeral" or "That Benny Olson was sort of an odd character" or "My grandma knew the Helgersons in Mt. Sterling."

The preponderance of opinion is along the same lines. "Erdman Olson got this girl pregnant, and didn't want to marry her, so he killed her, and skipped the country." Country as meaning leaving the area, not necessarily moving to a country outside the United States.

What happened to Erdman Olson? Speculation remains rife. People had Erdman going to Canada, to Mexico, to South America, back to his ancestral home of Norway, enlisting in the Navy, working tobacco farms down South, working on ranches out West, and shipping out as a crew member of a seagoing freighter.

Another intriguing possibility has been raised by several men well versed in understanding human psychology. They have studied the descriptions of his character taken from friends in the Seneca, Mt. Sterling, and Rising Sun area, plus descriptions given by his classmates at Gale College. Add that testimony to his previous shooting of a boyhood friend, the fact that he carried a revolver, at a time when no one else carried a gun.

An area funeral director, who has written accounts of various southwestern Wisconsin murders, believes that Erdman most likely gravitated to a large city, changed his name, perhaps hair style, and became involved in one of the flourishing urban organized crime syndicates.

An area historical society president is of the same opinion. He thinks Erdman fled as far away from the Midwest as possible and got lost in a big city, such as Los Angeles.

The Thomas Melvin family lived on the same road as the Albert Olson farm. Today that road is called Lone Pine Lane, the road to the John and Susan Oppreicht farm.

"Young Melvin said they saw a car pull into there several times, stay a few days, then leave," a resident of the area told this author. Did Erdman Olson come back to visit his parents, Albert and Anna Olson, and his brother, Arvid? There is no proof, but is seems inconceivable that Erdman Olson did not return to visit his family at some point.

It became known several years after the murder that the sheriff had asked that all mail delivered to the Albert Olson family be screened carefully by the rural mail carrier out of Ferryville. That mail surveillance went on for several years, but nothing of value was ever intercepted.

If Erdman was not stopped by a patrolman for a traffic violation or equipment failure, such as a burned-out headlight, and did not stop for gasoline in any nearby town, there is no reason he could not slip in and out of the Olson farmstead without anyone knowing.

If the Melvin family suspected that Erdman Olson was visiting his parents, why didn't they alert the authorities? Perhaps they thought young Erdman was not guilty, that "he had been hounded out of the area by Chris Olson who sicced the sheriff on him." (Note: sic is a slang expression meaning "to set a person to pursue.") A number of people reasoned along the same lines.

In their quiet moments alone, what did Albert and Anna Olson say to each other about their firstborn son? Surely, there must have been doubts about Erdman's innocence. The letter from Erdman to Clara, recovered from her tomb on Battle Ridge, was a virtual confession. The instructions were to burn all the letters, bring as much money as she could, and attend the dance in Seneca to establish an alibi. If innocent, why did he run? Did they wonder the same thing that Chris Olson asked? Why were there no letters sent by Erdman to Clara after September 7? Was it because Erdman knew she was dead?

Reporters periodically visited Chris and Dina Olson on their farm off Stony Point road. In 1929, three years after the murder and burial of Clara Olson, a reporter interviewed Chris Olson in the rambling farmhouse a few miles northwest of Seneca. A summary of the newspaper article follows:

"I did find out some things," he said. He remained obsessed with the idea of finding Erdman, using all the money available from his farm in an unrelenting search for the young man who killed his daughter Clara, threw her in a hilltop grave, then disappeared.

He kept numerous letters stuffed in folders and pigeonholes in an old desk. Tips come in from "people who know something." He followed up on every possible lead and sighting.

"If only I had the money, I would get that fellow," he confided to a reporter. Olson did not get any help from the district attorney or the sheriff. Crawford County offered a generous bounty, but that would be paid only when Erdman was caught. No monies were available from the authorities for hiring private investigators.

Olson claimed he spent more than $1,000 hiring detectives. Leads had dried up, and as time went on, it seemed that Erdman was safe from the reach of the law. The hue and cry had died. No really good photographs of Erdman Olson had been sent out. No adequate descriptions of the killer had been released or broadcast. Members of the Chris Olson family were convinced that authorities had not done enough.

The sons were willing to help. But for their willingness, Chris might have long since given up the hunt. Their toil made the hiring of farm help unnecessary, and their wages largely went to pay the expenses of the search. Bernard had gone on long trips at a moment's notice to view some suspect. He had been to Iowa, to Wisconsin cities, and to a farm near the Canadian border.

Chris told a reporter, "Two men drove into our farmhouse at dusk one night. They had come 800 miles from the northwest. A young man answering the description of Erdman Olson was working on a farm, and they want someone to identify him. Bernard put on his coat and rolled away in the dark with two strangers. He came back two days later by train. I know these fellows all right for the boy to go with them." Yet Bernard returned to report another false lead.

The dream that Chris told reporters that he had about "seeing" Clara buried face down in grave on Battle Ridge had come back to haunt him in a strange sort of way. He received several letters, mailed at different points in Wisconsin, that he believed came from Erdman.

They accused him of slaying both Erdman and Clara and called upon him to confess. This was a favorite theory of long-distance sleuths. The letters mocked law officers for failing to recognize Chris Olson as a guilty person. After all, how could Chris Olson know so many details of the murder unless he committed the crime himself? The accusations angered the aged tobacco farmer.

"That boy is not smart. If he was smart, he would have written Clara a letter as soon as he got back to Gale college, after her death. If that letter came here, just like nothing happened, well, he might've even fooled me."

Every clue ever offered by mail had been saved by Olson. His old desk fairly bulged with the overflow. He opened it so often that he could skim through the letters in a jiffy and produce the one he wanted. Chris would not part with them so that a comparison can made by handwriting experts.

"I know these letters they are from him," Olson told a reporter. The letters from Erdman were closely guarded. A reporter wrote, "To an unscientific observer, the anomalous letters are very similar penmanship and also bear resemblance in certain idiosyncrasies to letters which Erdman wrote to Clara." Chris Olson's unwillingness to turn the letters over to a handwriting expert was strange, though. If he was willing to go to the ends of the earth and spend big bucks to track down

Erdman, why didn't he release the letters to professionals? The answer, sadly, may be that he knew they weren't real. He held onto them because at least they offered the last flickers of hope.

On the other hand, why would Erdman ever write letters to the father of the young lady he killed? Fingerprinting was becoming a staple tool of law enforcement. Postmarks could be traced to locations. It is beyond belief that Erdman would take any chance, or have any reason, to write a letter to Chris Olson.

The very atmosphere about Chris Olson breeds suspicion. To visiting reporters, he mentions characters in the tragedy. He recounts incidents involving them, points out the significance of acts and chance remarks. The visitor, leaving, finds himself strongly suspecting that there may be foundations for some of the old farmer suspicions and wondering why the odds and ends of evidence detailed by Chris have not been run down.

Letters still drift from distant places to the Olsons, to the district attorney, to the sheriff offering "clues." Erdman has been seen here and there. Bernard is still trying to go out of the way to identify new suspects. The unrelenting quest of Chris that his son goes on and on from the Olson farmhouse on a windswept hilltop. "Feelers" reach out over the countryside for more and more fragments of information on the Olson murder case. Chris Olson has sunk his teeth in this case and will not let go.

The tragic aftermath of murder is the one left behind. Chris Olson would continue to seek out any news that would allow him to put to rest the unforgivable death of his daughter. The seasons would pass. Fields of tobacco would ripen and dry in their predictable cycle. But the rupture caused by the loss of his precious Clara would never be made right.

What Happened to the Families?

What happened to the Chris Olson family?

Minnie, oldest daughter, nearing her mid-30s, went back to work at a La Crosse hospital. She did not marry and lived until 1981.

Adolph lived until 1972, dying at age 80. He reportedly lived with his sister, Alice at Dane, Wisconsin, north of Madison.

Bernard (Bennie) and his brother Adolph, eventually took over the family farm. Neither Olson boy married, and they kept separate bank accounts.

Emma died young at age 57.

Arthur married and had three children and lived in the Milwaukee area.

Alice, Clara's younger sister by three years and closest confidant, became a nurse's aide in La Crosse. She married Maxwell Stevens in 1944. They had a son, Richard Stevens.

Cornelia, born in 1909, married Marvin Thompson. They had a son named Albert Thompson and lived in Fremont, Wisconsin, in Waupaca County, with burial in Hitterdahl Cemetery, near Iola, in Waupaca County.

Inga, born in 1913, was 13 years old when her older sister Clara was bludgeoned to death in 1926. She married a Scribbens, and they had five children. A son, John, lives in the Richland Center area.

Chris Olson lived a full life to age 81, passing away in 1948. He spent 22 years searching for his daughter's killer but to no avail. His wife, Dina, passed away in 1944. She went to her grave believing she should have been firmer with Clara.

This Olson clan—parents, Chris and Dina, and four daughters, Minnie, Emma, Clara, Alice, and three sons, Adolph, Bernard, and the baby Arthur Edward—are all buried in the cemetery of Utica Lutheran Church.

At Utica Church, all these graves all in a line: Minnie (1892–1981), Adolph (1894–1972), Bernhard (1896–1982), Emma Kristine (1898–1955), Clara Dorthea (1904–1926), Alice Stevens (1907–1984), Arthur E (1905–1905), Inga (1913–1996) no headstone, Arthur (1902–1972), was buried in Milwaukee, and Cornelia (1910–) buried in Fremont.

The Chris Olson farm out on Stoney Point Road was large, consisting of 317 acres. It stretched down into Copper Creek, but did not have much tillable land. The Kenzie family bought it in 1979 and have a flourishing business, Stoney Point Flowers. They ship flowers all over the world.

The Albert Olson family also carried on. When Erdman disappeared, 11-year-old Arvid remained as the only child of Albert and Anna Olson. Albert was 43 years old at the time of the 1926 Clara Olson murder. He died in 1944 at the age of 61. His widow, Anna, lived until 1973.

Members of the Albert Olson family are interred in the cemetery at the South West Prairie Lutheran Church that the family attended for many years.

Arvid married Charlotte Zitzner in 1942 and took over the Albert Olson family farm due to the failing health of his father. Arvid and Charlotte raised four daughters. A son died in infancy. One of the daughters and her husband own and operate the farm at the present time.

By all accounts Arvid was a very decent human being, friendly, outgoing, strong leader, good husband and father. It was said by many that Arvid was "a top-notch" farmer. Given what he knew—the murder his brother was accused of, the talk and whispers, the inquest in Prairie du Chien—it could not have been easy making his way in the world. It was also said by a few people that Arvid took some secrets to the grave with him.

Clara lies in the Utica Church cemetery, along with her parents and other family members. The fog still owns the night in those hills and valleys, but when the burning sun rises, the fog is burned off, and all is clear. The memory of this heinous crime is still part of the folklore of the hills. The mystery of Erdman's disappearance remains shrouded in darkness and fog. Did he start a new life in some faraway place? Did he kill again? Did he tire of running and end it all? The many wooded bluffs, caves, and swamps in the Kickapoo region keep their secrets.

Our society in these modern times places a lot of stock in winners and losers. Not only in sports, of course, but also in our political situations where newspeople are constantly informing us of who is "up" and who is "down" for any given occasion or event.

There are no winners in this calamity. Recall Rev. Finstad's sermon at the December 7, 1926, funeral for Clara Olson at the hilltop Utica Lutheran Church. "This is a tragedy for both families," Rev. Finstad pronounced.

Recall the weeping Chris Olson lying on his couch having just returned from Mt. Sterling on December 2 and identifying the corpse of his daughter Clara. "My family is better off now than his is, even if my little Clara is gone," he cried.

Clara's family has some contentment of knowing where Clara is, what happened to her, and who was responsible. There is no joy in this satisfaction. But consider the consequences of not finding Clara up there on Battle Ridge, of never knowing where she was, or what happened to her. That would be an emptiness, a gnawing of the soul and psyche that would never go away. There was some kind of closure for the Chris Olson family.

The Albert Olson family also lost a son. Erdman may or may not have returned to visit the home farm. It is quite likely Erdman never did contact his parents and his brother, Arvid. The Albert Olson family may have gone to their graves wondering, wondering, wondering. The words of Chris Olson resonate: "My family is better off now than his is, even if my little Clara is gone."

Timeline

Summer 1925. Erdman meets Clara at Lutheran Church social.

April 1, 1926. Clara Olson pregnancy occurs about this time.

August 17. Clara writes letter to Albert Olson, Erdman's father, she is 4–5months pregnant.

September 7. Erdman writes letter to Clara. She receives it in the mail on September 9.

September 9. Clara receives letter from Erdman, instructions on what to do that night.

September 9. Erdman digs grave in the afternoon.

September 9. Clara leave home late at night. Leaves note for parents. Never seen alive again.

September 9. Erdman Olson leaves dance in Seneca at 11:35 PM.

September 9. Chris Olson, father, hears Clara leave, she jumps in car.

September 10. Fri. Clara missing from her house. Chris Olson sends his son, older brother Bernard, to visit Erdman.

September 12. Sun. Erdman goes back to college at 8:30 PM. Edwin Knutson drives.

September 24. Fri. Christ and Dina visit Albert Olson family. Learns Clara is 5 1/2 months pregnant.

September 26. Sun. Chris Olson and two Helgersons visit Erdman at Gale College. Erdman writes and mails two letters, one to his father Albert, and one to Chris Olson, Clara's father.

September 26. Sun. Chris Olson has dream that Clara is dead.

September 27. Monday. Erdman visits college president. Erdman leaves school and is never seen again.

September 29. Wed. Erdman Olson's parents get letter "You'll never see me again. ..."

September 29. Wed. Chris Olson gets letter from Erdman: "Your daughter will come back."

September 29. Wed. Albert Olson's visit the Chris Olson's after receiving letter from their son, Erdman plus the *Tribune* story. First time Albert meets Chris.

September 29. Wed. Chris Olson hires two detectives, John Sullivan, retired Milwaukee Chief of Detectives, and Madison private detective, Caswen, a retired police detective.

Mid November. Chris Olson visits Albert Olson farm a second time, talks to Albert Olson.

November 25. Thurs. Thanksgiving. Chris and two detectives confer with newly elected Sheriff Harry W. Underwood and District Attorney J. S. Earll.

November 26. Fri. Chris Olson files murder complaint with Crawford County. Swears out a warrant.

November 27. Sat. Farmers' posse begins searching.

November 30. Tues. Judge C. H. Speck issues warrant for Erdman's arrest for murder. Story hits newspapers.

November 30. Tues. Chris Olson offers $200 reward.

December 1. Wed. *Chicago Herald Examiner* first stories. On wire services.

December 2. Thurs. Widespread search begins. Clara Olson found buried in grave, 10:30 AM. Coroner arrives. Body to funeral home in Mt. Sterling. Chris Olson identifies body. Body goes to Otteson Funeral Home in Prairie Du Chien for autopsy.

Letter from Erdman to his parents released, full text, late Thursday night.

December 3. Fri. District Attorney J. S. Earll comes home Friday from Chicago to take charge of the investigation.

December 4. Sat. Dr. Bunting arrives in morning by train, three hours autopsy, then body taken to family home near Seneca. Sheriff Harry Sherwood returns from Chicago. Inquest: pathologist and doctors.

December 6. Mon. Inquest held all day. 500 people came. Jury names Erdman as killer after 10 minutes after close of testimony.

December 7. Tues. Clara Olson burial at Utica Lutheran Church, known as Norwegian Lutheran Church. 600 people attend.

December 7. Tues. People start raising $5,000 as reward for Erdman Olson capture.

December 10. Fri. Edwin Knutson questioned.

February 2, 1927. James Holmes suicide, shot in heart, hollow tree, Kickapoo Valley.

March 27, 1927. Wedding clothes, cardboard box found near grave.

June, 1928. Albert Olson asks governor for court review.

1940. Reward money turned back into the Crawford County general budget.

Acknowledgments

Jake Vedvik, teacher Seneca and Crawford County historian

Dennis Wilson, Lancaster, Grant County historian, *Murder of a Good Daughter*

Susie Kenzie, lives on Chris Olson farm

Roger Forde, Shanghai Ridge—Rising Sun native, Wauzeka rural mail carrier

Judith E Hanson, Mt. Sterling

John Scribbins, Richland Center

Keith Cook, Galesville historian

Dorothy Gilkes, Prairie du Chien

John H. Sime, Readstown funeral director, writer for *Epitaph-News*

Dorothy M Briggson, Viroqua

Mary Elise Antoine, president of Prairie du Chien Historical Society

Janet Geisler, Crawford County Clerk

Russ Dennison, professor and chair of Library Department, Winona State University

Michael Lesy, author, *Murder City, Christ's Dream*

James J. Colby, *True Detective Magazine*, May 1930

American Weekly, Inc., 1928 MORE MYSTERY IN CLARA OLSON'S MYSTERIOUS MURDER

Dennis Pelock, Crawford County Highway Commissioner

Larry Quamme, Crawford County History Society President

John Paine Editorial Services

Newspapers

Prairie du Chien Courier Press

La Crosse Tribune-Leader Press R. L. Bangsberg

Chicago Herald Examiner, Harold L. Polland

Winona Republican Herald

Chicago Daily Tribune, Orville Dwyer

Sheboygan Press Roy J. Gibbons

Milwaukee Sentinel J. J. Colby

People Involved

Albert Olson family

Christ Olson family

Captain John Sullivan, retired Milwaukee Chief of Detectives, secret service agent

William Caswen, Madison retired police detective

C. H. Speck, Justice of the Peace

Harry W. Sherwood, sheriff 1924–1926

Emmet L. Haggerty, sheriff 1927–1928

A. N. Scoville, sheriff, 1929–1932

J. S. Earll, Crawford County District Attorney

Arthur Curran, District Attorney, elected 1926

Frank S. Holly, Coroner

Ernest Otteson, Coroner, elected 1926

Oliver and Andrew Helgerson, Mt. Sterling residents

Merle Murray, Mt. Sterling farmer

Park Morris, proprietor of Mt. Sterling Hotel

K. Lokensgard, President of Gale College, Galesville, WI

Orville Dwyer, *Chicago Daily Tribune*, star correspondent

Harold L. Polland, *Chicago Herald and Examiner*, writer

Hamilton R. Bailey, *Chicago Herald Examiner*, human interest stories

Charles A. Bonniwell, Character analyst and psychologist

R. L. Bangsberg, *La Crosse Tribune*, writer

James J. Colby, *Milwaukee Journal*, writer

Dr. Francis Gerty, Chicago, expert on dreams, Chicago's Cook County Hospital.

Paul Dommersnaes, Mt. Sterling funeral home director

Nels Severson, uncle of Erdman Olson, owner of land of burial site

Dr. Charles H. Bunting, pathologist at the University of Wisconsin

Dr. C. A. Armstrong, Prairie du Chien physician

Dr. J.J. Kane, Prairie du Chien physician at the sanitarium

Dr. F. J. Antoine, Prairie du Chien physician

Christine Anderson, Erdman Olson dance partner

Marie Anderson, Erdman Olson dance partner

Rev. Finstad, Lutheran minister at Utica Lutheran Church

Rev. Martin Dommersnaes of Soldiers Grove